Teaching Hemingway and Race

TEACHING HEMINGWAY

Mark P. Ott, Editor

Susan F. Beegel, Founding Editor

Teaching Hemingway's *The Sun Also Rises*
EDITED BY PETER L. HAYS

Teaching Hemingway's *A Farewell to Arms*
EDITED BY LISA TYLER

Teaching Hemingway and Modernism
EDITED BY JOSEPH FRUSCIONE

Teaching Hemingway and War
EDITED BY ALEX VERNON

Teaching Hemingway and Gender
EDITED BY VERNA KALE

Teaching Hemingway and the Natural World
EDITED BY KEVIN MAIER

Teaching Hemingway and Race
EDITED BY GARY EDWARD HOLCOMB

Teaching Hemingway and Race

Edited by Gary Edward Holcomb

The Kent State University Press   Kent, Ohio

© 2018 by The Kent State University Press, Kent, Ohio 44242
All rights reserved
Library of Congress Catalog Card Number 2018008746
ISBN 978-1-60635-357-8
Manufactured in the United States of America

Library of Congress Cataloging-in-Publication Data
Names: Holcomb, Gary Edward editor.
Title: Teaching Hemingway and race / edited by Gary Edward Holcomb.
Description: Kent, Ohio : The Kent State University Press, 2018. | Series: Teaching
    Hemingway | Includes bibliographical references and index.
Identifiers: LCCN 2018008746 | ISBN 9781606353578 (pbk. : alk. paper)
Subjects: LCSH: Hemingway, Ernest, 1899-1961--Study and teaching. | Race in
    literature. | Race relations in literature.
Classification: LCC PS3515.E37 Z89173 2018 | DDC 813/.52--dc23
LC record available at https://lccn.loc.gov/2018008746

Contents

Foreword
    MARK P. OTT   vii

Acknowledgments   ix

Teaching Hemingway and Race: An Introduction
    GARY EDWARD HOLCOMB   1

Reading Between the (Color) Lines: Teaching Race in Hemingway's "The Battler"
    MARC DUDLEY   7

Teaching Hemingway Short Stories through the Lens of Critical Race Theory
    MARGARET E. WRIGHT-CLEVELAND   16

Hemingway's Experts: Teaching Race in *Death in the Afternoon* and *Green Hills of Africa*
    ROSS K. TANGEDAL   29

Racial Politics to Social Action: Teaching Self/Other Dilemma in Hemingway's Works
    MAYURI DEKA   41

Blooming Hemingway
    CAM COBB AND MICHAEL K. POTTER   53

Mexicans in Montana: Teaching Hemingway and *Los Betaleberos* in "The Gambler, the Nun, and the Radio"
    SARAH DRISCOLL   74

Teaching the Harlem Renaissance through Hemingway: Divergences and Intersections of *The New Negro* and *In Our Time*
    CANDICE PIPES   85

Lost in Transition: Questions of Belonging in Hemingway's "Soldier's Home" and Hughes's "Home"
    JOSHUA M. MURRAY   98

A Classroom Approach to Black Presence in *The Sun Also Rises*
    GARY EDWARD HOLCOMB   105

Teaching the Pastoral and Race in Jean Toomer, Ernest Hemingway, and Ernest Gaines
    MATTHEW TEUTSCH   114

Works Cited   123
Selected Bibliography   131
Contributors   134
Index   136

Foreword
Mark P. Ott

How should the work of Ernest Hemingway be taught in the twenty-first century? Although the culture wars of the 1980s and 1990s have faded, Hemingway's place in the curriculum continues to inspire discussion among writers and scholars about the lasting value of his work. To readers of this volume, his life and writing remain vital, meaningful, and still culturally resonant for today's students.

Books in the Teaching Hemingway series build on the excellent work of founding series editor Susan F. Beegel, who guided into publication the first two volumes of this series, *Teaching Hemingway's* A Farewell to Arms (2008), edited by Lisa Tyler, and *Teaching Hemingway's* The Sun Also Rises (2008), edited by Peter L. Hays. In an effort to continue to be useful to instructors and professors at high schools, community colleges, and universities, the newest volumes in this series are organized thematically, rather than around a single text. This shift attempts to open up Hemingway's work to more interdisciplinary strategies of instruction through divergent theories, fresh juxtapositions, and ethical inquiries, often employing emergent technology to explore media beyond the text.

Gary Holcomb's *Teaching Hemingway and Race* speaks to issues that continue to be of intense interest to students and scholars today: How did Hemingway engage challenging topics of ethnic, nonwhite, and tribal characters in his texts? And how do we teach the difficult topic of racial representation in his work? Holcomb's volume provides a range of pedagogical approaches to teaching Hemingway's writings with a view toward showing students how to understand the author's representations of ethnic, tribal, and international difference. Rather than suggesting that Hemingway's portrayals of cultural otherness are incidental to teaching and reading the texts, these essays bring to the fore such racial matters. Indeed, one of the aims of this book is to find common ground between writings by black authors and Hemingway—the white modernist—showing that, far from there being two worlds—one occupied by white modernists and the other by black—modernist literature formed a cosmopolitan conversation and intercultural kinship, an exchange of ideas and style. These essays not only place racial markers in their historical context but also illuminate those connections in useful ways for scholars, classroom teachers, and students. Readers will find it refreshing and interesting to encounter essays that put Hemingway's work alongside Alain Locke's *The New Negro*, and explore his influence on such figures as Jean Toomer, Langston Hughes, Ralph Ellison, and Ernest Gaines.

The expertise and insight Holcomb brings to his highly regarded, wide ranging scholarship on the Harlem Renaissance and such figures as Claude McKay, Hughes, Richard Wright, and Chester Himes are manifest throughout this volume. Holcomb brings forth a diverse range of essays that not only explore Hemingway's fiction through the lens of race but also revise our understanding of the complex cultural web that stimulated his imagination and his writing.

Indeed, this volume demonstrates that Hemingway's work is being taught in more thoughtful, creative and innovative ways in today's classrooms and lecture halls than ever before and that his work continues to inspire vigorous debate and insightful discussion now more than ever.

Acknowledgments

I would like to express my gratitude to the Hemingway Society for arranging the panel "Teaching Hemingway and Race," held at the Seventeenth Biennial Hemingway Society Conference, in Oak Park, Illinois, in July 2016, as well as the session on "Hemingway and Black Writers" for the Sixteenth Biennial Hemingway Society Conference, in Venice, Italy, in June 2014. Both sessions helped enormously in stimulating interest among potential contributors as well as classroom instructors for a pedagogically oriented textbook dedicated to the complex matter of teaching Hemingway with regard to race.

I am also indebted to Will Underwood, former director and current acquiring editor of Kent State University Press, and Joyce Harrison, former KSUP acquiring editor, for their encouragement and valuable contributions to the publication of this book.

In addition, I would like to thank Ohio University for a spring 2017 sabbatical, which assisted in finalizing the present project.

And, finally, I would like thank Kim Holcomb. This book would not exist if not for Kim's support.

Gary Edward Holcomb

Teaching Hemingway and Race

An Introduction

Gary Edward Holcomb

The intention of this textbook is to provide the college or high school instructor with a pedagogical approach to teaching Hemingway as issues of race inflect his writing. The most influential discussion of Hemingway and race occurs in novelist Toni Morrison's 1992 *Playing in the Dark: Whiteness and the Literary Imagination*. Morrison states that an American literary canon was established as a consequence of the formation of U.S. nationalist discourses. Imbued with white supremacist ideologies, American exceptionalist ideology demanded a national literature that manifested a unique, that is to say, white, spirit (6). The introduction of *Playing in the Dark* articulates the theory of the textual "Africanist presence" (5–6), an absence of black agency in literary texts that linguistically, through the act of disowning native sons and daughters, draws attention to a black spectral presence. Morrison's white, mostly male subjects are Faulkner, Melville, and other major American writers, including, and perhaps most critically, Hemingway, in company with the uncritical veneration built around the canonical author, his life, and his writing.

Relatively more recent critical discussions of Hemingway and race, however, have questioned the idea that black existence is so eloquently "absent" in Hemingway's writing. Richard Fantina's *Ernest Hemingway: Machismo and Masochism* (2005) argues that Morrison's take tends to trim down a thorny topic (137). Relying on, yet in critical tension with, Morrison's notion of an expressive black absence, Amy L. Strong's *Race and Identity in Hemingway's Fiction* (2008) examines "how Hemingway's fiction looks if we bring his nonwhite characters out of the background" (12). In *Hemingway, Race, and Art:*

Bloodlines and Color Lines (2011), Marc Dudley sees the literary product of the white American author's infatuation with Africa as an artistic act that both reassures and disconcerts white consciousness. Dudley argues that Hemingway's concern for race was a sign of a national unease about racial transformation, and he concludes that the white author's representations of race are not simply parsed. They are, again in tension, simultaneously a reinforcement of accepted beliefs and an interrogation of whiteness.

My own *Hemingway and the Black Renaissance* (2012), questions now accepted ideas about the white modernist and race by citing the voices of noteworthy black authors who have identified Hemingway as a major influence and considers how they put Hemingway's textual models to use. Essentially, my interest is in asking whether Harlem Renaissance writers (such as Langston Hughes, Claude McKay, Wallace Thurman, and Gwendolyn Bennett), as well as interwar and postwar authors (like Richard Wright, Chester Himes, Ralph Ellison, and Albert Murray), and contemporary writers (Gayl Jones and Derek Walcott) display a kind of literary double consciousness when they explicitly name Hemingway as a major inspiration and when they draw on the white author's existentialist themes and minimalist techniques for their own writings. What these authors universally esteem in Hemingway's writings, in spite of his occasional objectionable racial representations, is the way he portrays reality in a tangible and honest manner through the conventions of modern literary fiction.

This collection intends to provide a practicable means for teaching the subject of race in Hemingway's writing and related texts, from how to approach ethnic, nonwhite international, and tribal characters, to how to teach difficult questions of racial representation, without apology for Hemingway's sometimes troubling representations of race. Because of the diverse approaches to the theme of teaching Hemingway and race, the book is laid out in two parts. The first section provides a range of pedagogical approaches to teaching Hemingway's writings with a view toward showing students how to read the author's representations of ethnic, tribal, and international difference. Rather than suggesting that Hemingway's portrayals of cultural otherness are incidental to teaching and reading the texts, these essays bring to the fore such racial matters. The next section considers Hemingway's work in conversation with writings by black authors. This unit is arranged with a view toward finding common ground between works by black authors and white modernists, showing that, far from there being two disparate worlds, modernist literature formed a cosmopolitan conversation and intercultural kinship, an exchange of ideas and styles.

One objective of this book is to provide ways to address disconcerting racial language in texts like Hemingway's "The Battler"—namely, Bugs's "polite nigger voice" (103). Perhaps more vexing than the appearance of racist language in some of Hemingway's writing is the question of whether black characters measure up to the masculine author's well-known inclination to venerate an admirably stoic and consequently tough male standard. Sam, the black cook in "The Killers," for example, remarks disparagingly about Nick Adams's attempt to save the fugitive heavyweight, Ole Andreson: "Little boys always know what they want to do" (220). Is the comment symptomatic of Hemingway's need to portray black males as essentially either cowardly or impotent? The contents of this collection offer strategies to assist the instructor in teaching the contemporary student reader, trained to read through the multicultural studies lens, how to work through troubling representations in Hemingway's writings.

In "Reading Between the (Color) Lines: Teaching Race in Hemingway's 'The Battler,'" Marc Dudley sees the memorable short story as defiant in the face of a prescriptive, single-minded reading. Dudley believes that teaching Hemingway demands having students see the political investment in art, and then compelling students to recognize "multiple selves at work in a text." He sees Hemingway as "an impressionist of sorts, painting character and landscape for striking sensory effect" and as "a reporter, a historian, and sometimes a political agitator, looking both to document and manipulate truth." In this way, Dudley's approach becomes an attempt to set students to discussing difficult texts like "The Battler" without discomfort, thereby allowing students to experience Morrison's concept of "unspeakable things unspoken" (1).

Margaret E. Wright-Cleveland's "Teaching Hemingway Short Stories through the Lens of Critical Race Theory" offers a pedagogical approach to *In Our Time* aimed at the sophomore, junior, and senior college levels, majors and nonmajors, in literature and cultural studies classes with an orientation in American Studies and Women's Studies. Wright-Cleveland's objectives are for her students to gain an understanding of the racial markers in historical context and to see the connections between racial images of the past and the present. Looking at stereotypes in Hemingway's works along with images that go beyond social labeling, her approach examines blackness as well as whiteness to provide students with a sense of how each continued to be determined. Most important, Wright-Cleveland shows students that what we discover in U.S. literature offers a means to explore the connection between blackness and whiteness in American culture and identity in Hemingway's writings.

For Ross K. Tangedal, teaching Hemingway's most celebrated nonfiction works may be a demanding chore, but the effort ultimately is worth it. In "Hemingway's Experts: Teaching Race in *Death in the Afternoon* and *Green Hills of Africa*," Tangedal discusses how students seek answers to questions about imperialism and other complex matters in Hemingway's two nonfiction books. Tangedal is confident that concentrating on race and narrative technique will make for a productive pedagogical moment: "Contextualizing race in both texts primes students for serious discussions of authority, power, authenticity, and narrative purpose, and with a little help from Hemingway's 'experts,' the texts can become more valuable to teachers and students alike."

Mayuri Deka's "Racial Politics to Social Action: Teaching Self/Other Dilemma in Hemingway's Works" suggests a pedagogy for teaching Hemingway's writing that may assist students in their social development. Concentrating on such works as *A Moveable Feast* and *A Farewell to Arms* through the prism of Self/Other racial politics, Deka proposes that the difficult mediation between the Self and Other apparent in Hemingway's relationship with America and other cultures is appropriate for learning about and learning through language and culture. What is more, such an approach makes for an effective exercise in developing students' prosocial conduct. The pedagogical approach in Deka's essay would aid in the development of students' compound "identity-contents," thus making students open to discovering "commonalities between the Self and Other based on universal affective states and life conditions." Students thereby may take tangible steps toward lessening the suffering of others and engaging in social change.

Relying on Bloom's Revised Taxonomy, Cam Cobb and Michael K. Potter's "Blooming Hemingway" poses the question of how educators might develop vigorous learning outcomes when teaching Hemingway's short story in order to cultivate experiences embedded in critical pedagogy. Cobb and Potter provide an explanation of what the fundamental aspects of education mean and then pose some broad questions about the meaning of learning outcomes, why educators should start with learning outcomes and context, what deep learning is, and why a critical pedagogy is important. Cobb and Potter hope that raising such questions will support instructors as they reflect on what they aim to achieve by teaching "The Doctor and the Doctor's Wife" or any other Hemingway story. Cobb and Potter demonstrate how a set of vigorous learning outcomes might be applied to offer students a chance to learn about "The Doctor and the Doctor's Wife" in a learning context based in critical pedagogy and using constructivist principles. This essay considers how the instructor may encourage learning outcomes in relation to pedagogical context as well as learning characteristics. It then delineates how to classify learning outcomes in order to offer students learning experiences that have been carefully constructed.

Sarah Driscoll's "Mexicans in Montana: Teaching Hemingway and *Los Betaleberos* in 'The Gambler, the Nun, and the Radio'" considers the Anglo author's short story in view of how it relates to Hemingway's fascination with Latin America. Driscoll points out that Hemingway is dedicated to relating the narratives of a Mexican community and its fight for survival in racist Montana, where an "economic crisis has driven a wedge between those who have and those who don't." This essay suggests that Hemingway exhibits a genuine understanding of Latin American migrants and their struggles and thereby creates the circumstances for Chicano peoples to locate themselves in his work: "As racial profiling continues to be an issue for the Chicano and Mexican immigrant populations in America today, Hemingway's story is a refreshing reminder of the social justice issues Latin Americans face in contemporary American society."

The next several essays place writings by Hemingway alongside those by black authors, starting with several seminal texts of the Harlem Renaissance. Candice Pipes's "Teaching the Harlem Renaissance through Hemingway: Divergences and Intersections of *The New Negro* and *In Our Time*" presents a pedagogical approach to reading Alain Locke's defining Harlem Renaissance treatise with Hemingway's seminal, genre-breaking short story collection. Pipes wishes to propose that teaching the two texts offers hands-on options for undergraduate as well as graduate instruction. *The New Negro* and *In Our Time* are useful for introducing both black and white modernisms, and together make an introduction to the "micro-affirmations" in Hemingway's texts countered by the "micro-inequities" in Harlem Renaissance texts. Through the comparative study of white and black modernist literature, Pipes believes that students will be provided with a practical sense of how to expand their own definition of modernism and thereby understand how black and white authors collectively played a role in the articulation of a transnational modernism.

Joshua M. Murray's "Lost in Transition: Questions of Belonging in Hemingway's 'Soldier's Home' and Hughes's 'Home'" arranges the white author's writing alongside that of a major Harlem Renaissance author, proposing that teaching Hemingway's and Hughes's stories together makes for a productive classroom discussion. Instructors and students may consider both the bond Hemingway had with Hughes as well as the sway the white modernist had on the Harlem Renaissance author as a budding fiction writer. Looking at these two stories in conversation permits the student reader to see the clear connection between the two modernist authors. Yet, the student reader may also see that rather than Hughes simply adopting the contour of Hemingway's story, translating the white protagonist into a black character, Hughes's story nuances his model.

The interesting result is that Hughes's "Home" so intimately emulates Hemingway's "Soldier's Home" that the disparate endings form a complex dialectical interchange on the subject of Hemingway and race.

Like Candice Pipes and Joshua Murray, my own "A Classroom Approach to Black Presence in *The Sun Also Rises*" suggests ways in which Hemingway's fiction holds a complex conversation with Harlem Renaissance texts. In my essay, I suggest this by offering a pedagogical approach, concentrating on the two minor African American characters who materialize in the narrative, both described in terms of racist signifiers: the drummer in the dance club and the prizefighter in the Vienna boxing ring. The conception that the racial language in *The Sun Also Rises* merely reflects white Protestant, middle-class American views during the 1920s is an insufficient approach. Rather than treating *The Sun Also Rises*'s minor black characters—black modern figures taken from Harlem Renaissance acts of identity making—as inconsequential, I highlight their presence as essential aspects of the novel. As a form of practical comparative literary study, I suggest instructors have students read Hemingway's novel in conversation with Claude McKay's novel *Home to Harlem* or Gwendolyn Bennett's short story "Wedding Day," two Harlem Renaissance texts that plainly hold difficult dialogues with *The Sun Also Rises*. Ultimately, students must learn how to work out the presence of masculinity as it traverses race and sexuality issues in the novel, and my essay offers an approach that deals with such issues.

Matthew Teutsch's "Teaching the Pastoral and Race in Jean Toomer, Ernest Hemingway, and Ernest Gaines" offers instructors a means for teaching how each author either deals with the issue of race or suggests its presence as a primary theme in their short stories. Teutsch argues that teaching Hemingway's "Big Two-Hearted River," Toomer's "Avey," and Gaines's "The Sky is Gray" "allows for a look not only into race and the way that the authors explore it but also at how they use the pastoral to comment on white and African American responses to the urban environment." While Hemingway steers clear of having Nick Adams come in contact with modernity, except in the form of Seney's remains, Toomer's and Gaines's characters confront the urban environment and what it means to be African American. Whereas Nick does not have to concern himself about the issue of race because he can locate his place in the world and be "happy," even with his traumatic memories of war, in Toomer's story, Avey, James, and Octavia are denied such a luxury due to their racial identity. They must face up to "the reality of history" that subjects them to racism and oppression.

Reading Between the (Color) Lines
Teaching Race in Hemingway's "The Battler"

Marc Dudley

Ernest Hemingway was very much a man of his time; he was also a man of his nation—robust, modern, unapologetically complex. "The Battler" is a wholly American story. Like several of his short works, this tale is unsettling, and therefore wonderful to teach. I must say that I am generally surprised each time I teach it, and the reasons are several: I am surprised by the number of students who have never heard of it, by the number who have never read it, and by the number who read it as everything but a story of race. I teach this story, generally, as a story of exploration, in which Hemingway mines and examines both American history and, necessarily, ideas of otherness.

I enjoy teaching this story for a number of reasons. First and foremost, it is one of his tightest, most mature stories, even as it comes early in his career. "The Battler" is a great example of the oft-noted "Hemingway style" at work—taut narrative, marked attention to physicality, and evocative dialogue. With his iceberg principle on full display, Hemingway is impressionistic and wickedly implicative. It is, I remind my students, often what Hemingway does *not* say that weighs most heavily on the page. However, getting students to see what is not there is often the greatest challenge.

All too often, at the sophomore survey level especially, students want desperately to see one answer, one prescriptive, when engaging a particularly troublesome, though seemingly simple text. Students look for the "right" answer in trying to decipher such texts. Or else, they wish to apply a universal reading to a text, often missing altogether the politics of gender, class, and race at work in a text. Surprisingly, many students, even those taking a more specialized, upper-level course like my American Author's, come to this particular story with very green eyes. Hemingway's texts, often pared down to an impossible gray—and "The Battler" is no exception—makes a singular reading nearly impossible. And therein, I remind my students, lies the challenge and the fun.

Race in particular often proves a difficult lens through which to read a work; and it proves difficult for a couple of salient reasons. First, head-on engagements with race can often be discomforting, sometimes because they are completely foreign entanglements. Second, and because of this first reason in particular, race quickly becomes that taboo subject that sits like an elephant in the middle of the classroom, silently but insistently biding its time while students find their way to it or altogether avoid it. I do not exaggerate when I say I have had many class discussions expressly centered on African American authors—renowned writers like Langston Hughes, Zora Neal Hurston, and Richard Wright—and the race card is never once played by a single student those first twenty minutes' worth of discussion. What makes this especially frustrating for me, given this broader discussion about teaching race in the classroom, is that these authors in particular had racial negotiation and matters of American social equity as a core part of their aesthetics throughout their respective careers; for them, race mattered. This point is often initially lost on many students who either fail to see or refuse to see the work as an exercise in racial politics. I should note that in almost every instance, those students caught completely unawares are white; while quite often, my students of color note the racial subtext at work. Indeed, interpretation is often very much a function of experience. I think the express silence on the matter is often attributable both to ignorance and privilege on the one hand, and deliberate, express political correctness on the other. Thus, it is a matter of getting students to see the politics invested in the art, and of forcing students to recognize the possibility of multiple selves at work in a text. Hemingway works as an impressionist of sorts, painting character and landscape for striking sensory effect; but he also works as a reporter, a historian, and sometimes a political agitator, looking both to document and manipulate truth for optimal psychic effect. It often becomes a matter of getting those same students to discuss comfortably what so many are afraid to mention for fear of flaring up latent sensitivities, to articulate what Toni Morrison calls those "unspeakable things unspoken."

As an easement of sorts, I begin with a general, but germane application of sociological theory to our discussion, segueing from talk of possible themes at work to a more nuanced examination of purpose. Here I introduce sociolinguist Norman Fairclough's assertion in *Language and Power* that all human interaction is undergirded by personal or communal agenda, that all social engagement is political in nature. The very act of communicating is an act of negotiation; in that act—whether consciously or unconsciously—we convey our wants, needs, and desires. In truth, artists, I argue, are especially often complicit in such social subterfuge. Hemingway's engagement with such subjects as race drives home this point.[1]

We get to this promised land of recognition through some subterfuge of my own, as I first engage student comments about the story's abject strangeness, its "bizarreness." The "bizarre" comments emanate from the scarred, misshapen, or else incongruous bodies we encounter in the text. In likening this story to any number of tales of the Southern Gothic (I often point to Flannery O'Connor, a name recognizable to many), I suggest that students read it as a "grotesque" story. Here I pause to define and then discuss the idea of the grotesque and underscore its purpose in literature, in its charge to shock the audience into recognition of special truths. I then ask students to explore with me what this story could be about more generally speaking.

My students often prove themselves to be quite adept at noting and discussing the story's possible general thematics: it is a story about friendship, many quickly remark. Others quickly note the violent temper that marks that friendship. To that end, we discuss it is as a story about such bonds framed within the brutality and violence of the world. The Hemingway universe is often brutal and unkind, I remind them. Others assert that it is about discovery, too. A young Nick Adams wanders the countryside by train and by foot and (re)discovers a childhood sport hero. I usually meet this claim with a suggestion about loss. While those losses of the former prizefighter are readily apparent (he is physically damaged), Nick's own losses, I suggest, are never enumerated, but they are also apparent (no family, friends, or personal backstory). Finally, I suggest that "The Battler" is also a story of survival. As the tale begins, the narrator assures us, "Nick stood up. He was all right." In fact, all of the tale's featured primary players are survivors. Nick makes his way through the midwestern landscape—one strewn with jagged edges, ominously dark spaces, and hardboiled realities—to the other side of the darkness to live another day.

The story ostensibly has a young Nick playing the part of vagabond and being discovered as a stowaway by the train's conductor. He is summarily tossed from the train as the story opens. He then makes his way to a makeshift camp inhabited by a wandering duo—former middle-weight boxing champion Adolph Francis and his companion/caretaker, Bugs. After openly welcoming Nick into the camp with talk of former glory, Ad rather quickly turns on him in an inexplicable act of violence near story's end. Ad's companion, Bugs, summarily knocks the man unconscious as he sets upon Nick, allowing the boy to escape unscathed and enlightened. The quieter moments are where the story's more salient elements live, and it is here where Nick's real discoveries are made. Here we discover the duo's individual histories and their shared past. Here, too, I tell my students, Hemingway reminds us of our own dark national history in the making.

To fully understand it all, I underscore Hemingway's genius in manipulating actual fact in forging his fiction. I draw students' attention to the litany of historically informed fictions in the Hemingway canon, beginning with titles at the tips of all their tongues and ending with those perhaps lesser known. *A Farewell to Arms, The Sun Also Rises,* and *For Whom the Bell Tolls* are all narratives steeped in the painful history of war, as are the tales from *In Our Time,* from which this story is taken. *Under Kilimanjaro,* his final fictionalized memoir, has, in limited relief, the Mau Mau uprisings in 1950s East Africa as its backdrop. I then point them to Hemingway's personal experience as a reporter for the *Kansas City Star* and the *Toronto Star* as further "proof" of his commitment to document history in the making. Michael Reynolds's *Hemingway's Reading, 1910–1940* demonstrates Hemingway's lifelong investment in things past. A look at Hemingway's collection of war-related histories and memoirs, with subjects ranging from Russian history to the American West's settling, underscores this point and becomes paramount in my mounting a case for this story being one very deliberately about race in early twentieth-century America.

I bring further evidence to bear as I remind my students that Hemingway was a writer by trade, a craftsman always working to hone his skills. I direct them to his many musings on writing in *A Moveable Feast,* his love letter of 1920s Paris memories. Hemingway assures us that truth telling for the writer involves one simple prescriptive: "All you have to do is write one true sentence; write the truest sentence that you know" (22). Ironically, I tell them, Hemingway begins writing that one "true sentence" in our featured story by bending the truth to fit his purposes, and here that purpose is a racial examination of his America. The text itself tells us so as Hemingway mines actual news headlines and injects his own fictions to make this a story expressly about race.[2]

I begin this portion of the class discussion by asking a couple of general questions. These questions are meant to acclimate students to the charged environs of a racial topography. I might begin the core portion of our talk by asking, "So how is this a story about race?" After all, one of the principal characters in "The Battler" is African American, and the pernicious N-word litters the story's literary landscape. Ninety percent of the time that elicits a trickle response, mostly intent on unilaterally branding Hemingway a racist, as students warm up to the idea of broaching the "R-word" portion of our conversation. Yet even those students intent on making allowances for the racist language will typically defend the writer as merely a product of his time. A typical defense might begin, "I agree that Hemingway's a racist, but. . . ." And the qualified case against a racist author builds momentum.

Taking their lead, I facilitate a dialogue that—at least at its outset—examines the story from this very perspective—Hemingway is, I agree, a man of his time, using the parlance of his day. But I concede this point only if my students are willing to go one further and ask themselves, "Why does he rely so heavily on the racial epithet, and why do so, so aggressively?" Our initial concession allows us then to examine the author through the bifurcated, racialized lens of early twentieth-century America. This marks a perfect opportunity to engage my students in dialogue about the racial ideas shaping the politics, the economics, the everydayness of many Americans almost a century ago. I find it striking the number of students unaware of racism's deep-seated presence in American life, outside of discriminatory laws and Jim Crow. Few are cognizant of the many race riots that erupted nationally during the new century's first decades; or the number of racially motivated lynchings committed during those years; or the damaging prevalence of biological determinism and eugenics that shaped popular thought; or the popularity and profound impact of the minstrel show; or the growing fear of boxer Jack Johnson in the world of big-money sports; or the truly galvanizing power and legacy of D. W. Griffith's *The Birth of a Nation*, a film sparking protests and racial violence across the country upon its 1915 release.[3]

Hemingway, I remind my class, lived this history. As historian and newspaperman, he would have noted all the aforementioned events, great and small, taking place both down the street from him and around the nation. As a boy, he would have been aware of the "science" (eugenics and phrenology were wildly popular among "scholars" and laymen alike) of the day. As a teenager, Hemingway would have noted the rise of Jack Johnson, the nation's first African American heavyweight boxing champion. In the years leading up to the publication of *In Our Time*, Hemingway would have been well aware of the racial strife plaguing the nation. Chicago, I suggest to my students, was the site of one of the nation's worst race riots just after Hemingway returned from war; and Chicago, I remind them, was ostensibly Hemingway's backyard, just eight miles from his hometown of Oak Park. Moreover, young Hemingway lived in a country separated by the color line; *Plessy v. Ferguson* became the law of the land only a few years before his birth. Finally, I concede, Hemingway was, as so many students assert, a man of his times. Those racial epithets peppering his texts would have been acceptable in many circles, including his own. But again, I ask them, what undergirds the aggressiveness of this parlance *here*?

I suggest to them the possibility of that aggressiveness being both a false flag and a deliberate directive by the writer. Hemingway wants us first to read the pronounced racial landscape, then, as always, to read between the topographical lines. For Hemingway, it is often the unsaid that is of greatest import. Here, aptly, a single racial marker does the work of twenty words. I underscore this point to my students as I have them count the number of epithets used in the story. Hemingway uses the word *negro* twenty-three times and the word *nigger* four in a story that spans less than ten pages. The two words are used interchangeably throughout the tale and done so with impunity. But *why?* In a word, effect. Perhaps no other singular word in the English language assumes such connotative power as that of the N-word. And Hemingway exploits this understanding like no one else, evoking and fashioning images from reader assumption. The word has divided a citizenry, provoked violence and even litigation, and continues to be the source of much discussion. Speaking of language's temporal nature, Supreme Court Justice Oliver Holmes noted almost a century ago that a word is "the skin of a living thought [that] may vary greatly in color and content according to the circumstances and the time in which it is used."[4] This brings us back to our original concession that Hemingway was indeed a man of his times; but I amend this claim in suggesting that Hemingway was a *writer* very much aware of his times and his countrymen. As Toni Morrison asserts of the N-word's inherent power in *Playing in the Dark: Whiteness and the White Literary Imagination,* "the spatial and conceptual difference is marked by the shortcut that the term 'nigger" allows, with all of its color and caste implications" (71). And Hemingway marshals the associative power of this word in fashioning the story's primary characters, Bugs and Ad.

As Hemingway crafts him, each man seems to be a "normative" representative of his race. At the outset, Hemingway constructs each character as type, each seemingly acting within the very tight racial confines of that narrative space demanded of him by contemporary white expectation. I ask students to tell me about each of the primary players as we meet him, reminding them that first impressions mean much. I ask, "How is Ad characterized when we first meet him?" I follow up with, "How does Hemingway characterize Bugs initially?" Our first impressions of Ad are Nick's own as we meet his sports hero, still embodying the endurance of Hemingway's "code hero." Students quickly note Nick's awestruck reaction to meeting Ad. While weathered, "misshapen," and "mutilated," this former champion is a survivor who boasts that while "They all bust their hands on me," opponents through the years "couldn't hurt me." While barely recognizable to Nick, Ad's big reveal ultimately elicits a giddy "Honest to God?" from him (99). Students then quickly recall how fit the former fighter is, despite his scary, busted form. Registering a heart rate of forty beats per minute, the former champion is still seemingly every bit the man he was years ago.

Conversely, broken countenance notwithstanding, students are quick to point out that Bugs appears more sinister overall than the misshapen ex-fighter. They point to his manhandling of Ad when the ex-fighter erupts in anger at Nick as a point of proof. To calm Ad, Bugs slugs him with the whalebone handle of a blackjack. Students sense a seemingly latent violence in Bugs, underscoring his having served time for "cuttin' a man" as further evidence for a case against him (103). Here I remind students that what we get is a constructed "blackness," and we get this from the outset. I remind them that Nick reads Bugs from afar, knowing the voice he hears in the darkness as "a negro's voice," and knowing "from the way [Bugs] walked that he was a negro" (100). This elicits comments about racial coding. Also, alternately, running counter to the knife-wielding thug image, is, simultaneously, that of the genial man-servant. Bugs is all deference and servility, embodied in the "long nigger legs" (100) he crouches on as he cooks for his two white compatriots. Thus, I demonstrate to students how Bugs quickly comes to counter all that Ad seems to be, encompassing two primary racial types haunting the contemporary white imagination: the "savage" bent on hyper-violence and the deferential man-child happy to serve. "Is this a fair and complete representation of Bugs?" I ask. I remind them this is merely part of the story. How then, I repeat, is this story a greater statement on race? Hemingway's grotesque tells us much.

Strong pulse or no, Ad Francis is a broken man, and his misshapen face attests to this fact. Further, his broken body acts as metaphor for a psychic brokenness. He tells Nick that he is "not quite right"; and as my students are quick to point out, he is in fact quite unstable, boastfully calling himself "crazy." When asked to produce further evidence of a man diminished, students begin to see that same pattern reveal itself; they then successfully mine the text for further evidence, pointing as proof to Ad's homelessness, his general dependency on his sister for money, and his dependency on Bugs, in general. I like to wrap up this part of our examination by directing students once more to the text's own literal diminution of this former great, having them note the narrative's repeated reference to Ad as the "little man."

And if we are to read these characters as part of a larger counter-narrative to the generally accepted racial chronicle, Bugs too becomes something wholly different from the early evocative, textual markers. My students are quick to point out that he is, in a very general sense, the last man standing at story's end, which, they insist, "probably means something." To that end, I add that of the two, Bugs is the calm, controlled (and controlling) agent. As opposed to Ad, who was jailed for being a loose canon of sorts, Bugs is very much in control of himself ("I hear most of what goes on" [100]), of Nick ("If you don't mind I wish you'd sort of pull out" [103]), and even of the former fighter ("I have to do it to change him when he gets that way" [102]). Most importantly, I assert, Bugs, not Ad, controls the narrative; after all, we learn about Ad's inglorious past through Bugs. Ad has the last word, not the formerly great (little) man.

To that end, I ask my students about boxing's import to this story. Why feature a former prizefighter as a principal character? And how could this fact lend itself to a reading on race? To the question of the sport, students quickly embark on a discussion of manhood as exemplified in the potentially brutal exercise. Here I suggest to them that boxing, much as was the case with baseball, was a sport of national interest. And equally important, like baseball, boxing was for some time primarily a white man's domain. Ad's diminution and Bugs's rise then take on special significance, especially when read through the lens of Jack Johnson, whose crossing of the color line inside and outside the ring made him a target for white America. While only a phantom here, Johnson's penchant for testing social mores is mirrored by Bugs who admits his affinity for "living like a gentleman" (103). And like Johnson, with veiled blackjack in hand, Bugs quietly threatens to upset the social order. At the very least, I insist to students, Hemingway questions that order.

When read this way, Hemingway's strange little piece becomes a striking interrogation of race relations at a time when unabashed racial dogma reigned supreme. Students are usually quite surprised when we arrive at this point in the discussion. At this juncture, I have them read, from the backs of their classroom editions of the text, Scribner's own open declaration regarding Hemingway's lasting influence: "Ernest Hemingway did more to change the English language than any other writer of the twentieth century." With "The Battler," I assert to my students, Hemingway cements his stature as modern with a textual exploration that is equally noteworthy for its substance as it is for its form. This, too, is part of Hemingway's enduring legacy.

Notes

1. I often include Hemingway's *To Have and Have Not* in my Hemingway seminar as an example of Hemingway the "experimenter." That novel demonstrates both Hemingway's interest in hard-boiled fiction and his investment in the socio-political (Depression-era economics are in his sights). Some scholars see it as an answer to critics who saw him as standing outside the political fray, pointing to *Green Hills of Africa* as a grand example. But "politics," I caution my students, are about more than "right" and "left" leanings; politics are agenda and interest-driven engagement. And in "The Battler," much of Hemingway's politics are racial. Thus, Kenneth Kinnamon's observation that "With few exceptions, Hemingway's biographers have discounted his interest in and understanding of politics" could not be any more astute (149).

2. Ever the keen observer, Hemingway made note of an actual contemporary news item involving a former lightweight champion fighter, Adolph Wolgast, and his caretaker in his later years, gym owner Jack Doyle. In actuality, both men were white. Hemingway rather conspicuously makes one of the men a black man in his fictional account. The truth of this story, I admonish my students, lies between the scripted lines and with authorial intention.

3. During the first two decades of the twentieth century, America saw racially charged violence in such cities as New York, Charleston, Knoxville, Washington, D.C., Norfolk, Omaha, Atlanta, and St. Louis. Some eight miles from Hemingway's hometown of Oak Park, Chicago, a city cited by Carl Sandburg as a model of diversity and progressive thinking as the century began, was no exception. It witnessed some of the worst violence of the so-called "Red Summer" of 1919. Incidentally, by this year, racial lynchings for the new century numbered well over a thousand.

4. See *Towne v. Eisner*, 245 US 425 (1918).

Teaching Hemingway Short Stories through the Lens of Critical Race Theory

Margaret E. Wright-Cleveland

Ernest Hemingway's hometown of Oak Park, Illinois, provided a complex understanding of race to a young man coming of age between 1899 and 1917. While consistently supporting laws to protect equality between the races and inviting African American leaders to speak, white Oak Parkers, in particular, struggled with what racial equality could look like outside of the courtroom and off the national stage in their own parlors and churches. During summers with his family and on his own in Petoskey, Michigan, from 1899 to 1920, Hemingway had access to images of race different from those in Oak Park. In Petoskey, Hemingway interacted with members of the Ojibwe tribe and read newspaper accounts of tawdry crimes painted with the hues of race and ethnicity, crimes that *Oak Leaves* would never have reported. Together, Petoskey and Oak Park provided Hemingway abundant contradictory lessons and images about a white man's place in the world and lay the groundwork for his ability to interrogate racial identity as a social construct. Whenever I teach *In Our Time*, I address the racial education Hemingway was exposed to in Oak Park and Petoskey. This text, in particular, demonstrates the varied ways Hemingway challenged the validity of the silent, invisible privilege of whiteness.

Images of blackness and whiteness exist everywhere in American culture: literature, film, music, advertising, sports, and daily conversation. Each generation creates some new images, alters other, and rejects some more. Still, historical racial images, of both blacks and whites, are persistent and persuasive, exerting influence over the role of race in American culture and in the formation of an

American identity. Investigating the racial education of Hemingway and how it might have influenced his writing enables students to question how their own racial education might be shaping them.

I have taught *In Our Time* to undergraduates at the sophomore, junior, and senior levels; to both majors and nonmajors; in literature classes and cultural studies classes, including American studies and women's studies. I always deal with the presentation of race Hemingway offers. My goals for my students include understanding the racial markers in their historical context, but also exposing connections between racial images of old and racial images of today. We look at images that established stereotypes and those that moved beyond stereotype. We examine blackness as well as whiteness in an attempt to understand how both have been and are still being defined. We consider how whiteness is used as a racial marker as blackness is and explore how white invisibility helps create white privilege. Most importantly, we use what we discover in America's historical literature to explore the nature of the connection between blackness and whiteness in all of American culture and in American identity, past and present.

Grounding Hemingway's inaugural work in the understanding of a racial education sets up four concepts important to the work of the class: all race is socially constructed; whiteness is a race; we learn the rules of racial construction in myriad overt and covert ways; all writers deal with race. Because there has been a historical assumption that white writers outside the South can choose to write about race or not, scholars and fans alike often do not expect Hemingway to write about race. To approach Hemingway through the lens of Critical Race Theory, students must first understand how race works in society, both theirs and Hemingway's. By examining historical cultural artifacts such as newspapers, letters, diaries, pictures, films, and legal documents, my students learn how the historical cultures of Oak Park and Petoskey presented themselves and influenced their citizens. This helps students better understand the implications of Hemingway's writing in his cultural moment.

Because Hemingway's texts continue to have a cultural presence, I ask my students to examine how their own society constructs race, ethnicity, gender, class, and nation. We then read Hemingway's stories against our current understanding of racial construction, asking if and how Hemingway's ideas on race are still relevant. Within all of our queries, we acknowledge that whiteness is a constructed racial category and one that Hemingway consistently interrogates.

Student investigation throughout the course cycles through these four questions:

- What was the racial education offered Hemingway by Oak Park and Petoskey?
- How did that racial education influence his work?
- What is the racial education being offered Americans today?
- What do Hemingway's stories offer to the current American conversation about race?

By working through cultural history, close reading of texts, and contemporary cultural analysis, students practice the un-silencing and re-visioning of still silent and invisible racial constructs. Holding Hemingway's stories to this scrutiny allows students to explore the power of language in ways that serves them as writers, readers, and citizens.

I begin all of my courses with the author's text. Immediately after the introductory meeting, students are required to read chapter one and "Indian Camp." I ask them to discuss what these stories tell us about race. Generally, students comment on the poor living conditions of the Native Americans and their need for the knowledge of white doctors trained in western medicine. Students usually don't offer a great deal of comment on chapter one and though they are embarrassed by the gross inequity between races and classes in "Indian Camp," they are unsure what Hemingway is doing with that inequity and what they, in turn, are supposed to get out of an inequity created generations ago. The next class I provide the following information about the racial education offered Hemingway in Oak Park.

Hemingway's First Racialized Community—Oak Park, Illinois

Few African Americans resided in Oak Park[1] before the Civil War. The post-Reconstruction period, the African American exodus north, and the Great Chicago Fire of 1871 brought many newcomers to Oak Park, both black and white, seeking jobs and the benefits of life in a suburban community. Anson Hemingway, Ernest Hemingway's grandfather, was one of those newcomers. In 1869, Anson brought to Oak Park his experiences as an officer with the Seventieth U.S. Colored Troops in Natchez, Mississippi, and the abolitionist stance he and his wife had embraced while at Wheaton College. The Hemingways' progressive understanding that black citizens should be equal under the law was welcomed in Oak Park. Anglo-American Reverend Joseph E. Roy, "a Congregationalist minister with a national reputation for his support of the abolitionist cause," was another racially liberal newcomer accepted by

Oak Parkers Roy held various national leadership positions in the American Missionary Association and the American Home Missionary Society, and published articles on race: "How to Overcome Race Prejudice" and "Our Indebtedness to the Negroes for Their Conduct during the War" (West et al. 5, 6). Publicly espousing a belief that blacks and whites should have equality under the law became part of Oak Parkers' identity, even before Ernest Hemingway was born.

Oak Park's racial progressivism was buttressed by state legislation. "In 1865 the Illinois Black codes were repealed, by 1870 blacks were granted the right to vote, and in 1874 the schools were desegregated. A state civil rights bill was passed in 1885 prohibiting discrimination in places of public accommodation" (West et al. 6). Immediately after Reconstruction, African Americans in Oak Park owned land, homes, and businesses. Though most African Americans worked in service areas or the skilled professions, some had education beyond high school and some were successful entrepreneurs. Will Palmer operated a teamster and hauling business and owned a boarding house "that served as a temporary home for newly arrived blacks while they sought work and permanent housing," some on their way farther north from the Deep South (West et al. 10, 11). The African American community in Oak Park after the Civil War became leaders of the nation in the repatriation of freed slaves and in modeling a successful working-class and middle-class lifestyle.

Since before the Civil War, Oak Park churches, black and white, functioned as hubs for defining and practicing racial identity. In 1893, the white congregation of Unity Church hosted Fannie Barrier Williams, a black female journalist and social reformer from Chicago, to give a public lecture. Williams was quoted in a Chicago newspaper the following week claiming she received a more hospitable welcome in Oak Park than she did in the all-white Chicago Women's Club. Williams would become the first African American member of the Chicago Women's Club—but not until 1896, three years after her warm reception in Oak Park (West et al. 6).

Oak Parkers consistently supported legal equality between the races, but true social integration was more difficult because it challenged long-held perceptions of whiteness. The building of the Mt. Carmel Baptist Church in 1905 became the first citywide controversy over the limits of racial integration. After years of saving, the fourteen members of the black congregation purchased land on which to build their sanctuary and published in the local newspaper a thank-you to the "many friends, both white and colored, who have so kindly assisted us" (*Oak Leaves* August 22, 1902: 8). However, some of the white neighbors who owned homes near the building site were not willing to have a black church and its congregants in their midst. City permits were offered and rescinded and the original site, purchased by the congregation for six hundred dollars, was sold to a group of white neighbors for nearly four times the purchase amount (West et al. 17). Eventually, support from prominent white Oak Parkers facilitated the selection of a new site, and the building of the first African American church in Oak Park was completed in 1905, when Hemingway was six years old. This compromise indicates the limits even prominent, progressive white Oak Parkers honored; they would work to redefine views of blackness, but they would not redress views that whiteness had power to choose its own neighbors. Such unwillingness or inability to confront flawed views of whiteness allowed the idea of white superiority to persist while ideas of black equality were growing. The ideas that whites can define the worth of blackness and that white superiority is not problematic are challenged in Hemingway's stories every time traditional definitions of white masculinity are challenged.

William E. Barton, Anglo American rector of the First Congregational Church, exemplified the contradictions progressive whiteness could maintain in order to avoid redefining itself. Reverend Barton publicly supported building the Mount Carmel Baptist Church and frequently advocated from the pulpit and the podium for equal rights for all races, but he also demonstrated an appreciation for the pseudo-science eugenics:

> I do not plead for social equality. I do not want to marry a negress. I have lived in the south and appreciate the problem of the south. And I can say there is but one solution of the negro problem, which is to let the negro become as much a man as his own ability and character will permit him. He will have a hard enough time trying to change the leopard's spots, some of which are native, some of them painted upon him by ourselves. But if by the grace of God he can bleach them a little, in the name of God help him. (qtd. in Reynolds, *Young Hemingway* 12).

Reverend Barton's views seem a fair representation of the various ways Oak Parkers could simultaneously embrace new views of blackness without relinquishing or even questioning old understandings of whiteness. Frank Lloyd Wright's daughter, Frances, had an African American best friend, Edith Palmer; the Oak Park-River Forest Boys Choir was an integrated choir (West 20); the local black community included businessmen, skilled craftsmen, a fireman, and an engineer, all of whom had white customers. The Nineteenth Century Club, a white women's organization dedicated to social betterment, focused on improving race relations beginning in 1904 and continued active involvement in racial equality groups through the 1920s. They created and financially supported the Elizabeth Charleton Day Nursery, proudly soliciting financial support from wealthy patrons with pictures of its integrated classes (*Oak Leaves* 2 May 1914). Yet, the integrated public schools failed to graduate an African American until 1923, six years after Hemingway graduated (West et al. 34). In 1908, the Forest Park Amusement Park opening included the African Dodger, a game in which patrons threw baseballs at a black man's head, and the African Dip, which featured black men on a dunk tank and the slogan "Hit a Coon and Win a Cigar!" (25). Public outcry over the violence of the "African Dodger" got it removed, but the African Dip continued. Minstrel shows were commonplace—both professional shows from Chicago and homegrown varieties to raise money for white church and civic groups—at the same time blacks and whites crowded into public halls to hear Booker T. Washington and Ida B. Wells-Barnett speak on achieving racial equality (28). Both blacks and whites energetically participated in and led civic organizations, but they did so separately; no civic group in Oak Park was integrated while Hemingway lived there.[2]

A particularly telling example of the difficulty liberal whiteness had in comfortably redefining itself and otherness is the report on the summer baseball game between the "academically educated white men" of Oak Park and the "the black boys composing the Leland Giants" (*Oak Leaves* 29 April 1914). To their credit, the Oak Park summer baseball league played black teams when other white teams would not, and white Oak Parkers paid to watch the competitions. Still, *Oak Leaves,* the only public voice of Oak Park, reported the game between the "black boys" and the "academically educated white men" as one enjoyed by "a good-sized crowd . . . for there always is comedy when colored men play ball. They improvise dialogs and monologs much to their own entertainment and also for the amusement of the spectators" (29 April 1914). Similarly, when progressive Oak Parkers visited Tuskegee, *Oak Leaves* reported the visitors "could not help but feel that he was in the midst of real, genuine American boys and girls despite their color" (4 March 1904). Michael Reynolds's 1986 analysis that Hemingway experienced merely the "benign racism" of his era demonstrates how difficult it is for whiteness to see its own privilege and power. No racism, regardless of how it is displayed, is benign. Racism in Oak Park may have avoided many acts of violence against African Americans, but it consistently demonstrated an ongoing struggle within the identity of whiteness. White Oak Parkers understood whiteness to be educated, American, and progressive. Progressive Oak Park whiteness *allowed* blackness access to education, American citizenship, and legal and social progress, but it did so without any sense it had to modify its role as sole arbiter of rights and identity. This schism between verbally arguing for the rights of blacks and refusing to give up the control of the dispensation of rights is a contradiction Hemingway noticed and demonstrated in his very first stories. The year Ernest Hemingway started high school, Oak Park experienced the most violent act of racism in its history: arsonists set on fire the home of the only black family in a white neighborhood, and any idea that Oak Park was without malignant racism or secure in its sense of whiteness was shattered (West et al. 31).

This historical look at Oak Park during Hemingway's childhood and adolescence models for students how to map cultural, racial education. For next class, I ask students to read chapter one and "Indian Camp" again and look for any evidence that Hemingway is addressing social racial construction. Inevitably, our second class discussion on these stories is buttressed with reading closely, exploring nuance, and questioning the roles of language, tradition, law, economics, and science in the construction of identity.

> Active Learning Project: Students are asked to collect ten cultural artifacts from the city they consider their hometown, the place in which they spent a significant portion of their formative years before attending the university, and create an Artifact Annotated Bibliography. These cultural artifacts may be statues, photographs, newspaper articles, advertisements for tourists, bumper stickers, T-shirts, websites, etc.—anything that presents information about or reflects some attitude of the community. For each artifact, the student is to provide a photo, copy, or description, the location in which this artifact was displayed, and an analysis of what it suggests about the racial constructions active in the community.

Before I provide background on Petoskey, I ask my students to read chapter two and "The Doctor and the Doctor's Wife." Our discussion, still informed by information about Oak Park, is rich. It will be richer the second time through, after I have provided students with the following information about historical Petoskey.

Lessons about Race from Petoskey, Michigan

Hemingway spent some part of every summer from 1900 to 1917[3] at Walloon Lake near Petoskey, Michigan. Petoskey was well established as a resort community by 1900 and hosted many "summer people" from Chicago. The Hemingways were typical of the "summer people" who would spend an extended period on the lakes of northern Michigan: middle- or upper-middle class, educated, white, predominantly Christian, and Republican. Part of Petoskey was Bay View, a Methodist meeting ground that could boast of 415 privately owned Victorian homes by 1900.[4] The Bay View Association of the Methodist Church hosted youth camps and adult meetings and, as part of the nineteenth-century Chautauqua network, provided a steady flow of speakers and musical concerts open to the community. Andrew C. Rieser effectively argues that the broad Chautauqua network expanded social understanding of whiteness to include multiple European ethnicities if they could perform patriotism along the lines described by the original Anglo-Saxonists.[5] This revised understanding of whiteness as not biologically based included only non-Asian and non-African ethnicities. Documents[6] advertising the Bay View Chautauqua events scheduled in the years the Hemingways were at Walloon Lake reflect a mindset consistent with Rieser's claims, "While white performers were billed as 'trained' and 'cultivated,' copy for black groups characterized them as rough-hewn talents of 'natural' spirituality and musicality whose stories came from the 'heart'" (148). Bay View reinforced Oak Park's image of whiteness as educated, progressive, and in charge of dispensing power and identity. We have no evidence Ernest Hemingway attended the Chautauqua events while visiting Petoskey, but we can surmise that information about speakers and reactions to their visits were readily available both in printed and verbal reports. Though more than likely Hemingway removed himself from any Chautauqua-like event, he lived in a community shaped by them.

Life on Walloon Lake was intentionally rustic, part of the contemporary cottaging movement that expected vacationers to "be more involved with the requirements of everyday life, including cooking and cleaning; more directly engaged with the natural world; and interact more with other family members" (Svoboda *Up North* 10). It provided for Hemingway much freedom to hike, hunt, fish, camp, and roam the woods without parental intervention, and Hemingway took advantage of this opportunity. At the turn of the twentieth century in northern Michigan, the woods also provided access to Native Americans and to a natural world at conflict with white human progress.

Financially destitute during Hemingway's time, the Ojibwe (or Chippewa) nonetheless brandished a proud history and an ability to adapt and survive that gave Hemingway another model for manhood. In 1887, Andrew J. Blackbird wrote the *History of the Ottawa and Chippewa Indians of Michigan*, and the Ypsilanti Auxiliary of the Women's National Indian Association published it. Blackbird, the son of the Ottawa chief, married a white woman of English descent, fathered four children with her, and worked for the U.S. government first as an interpreter and then as postmaster of Little Traverse, Michigan. Vetted with an introduction affirmed by nine white male leaders in Emmet County, Blackbird's book demonstrates the prevalent patriarchal attitude about Native Americans in the region both in content and in form.[7] Indeed, Blackbird had learned to be grateful that the white leaders of Michigan would treat tribal leaders as their own children: "For the Governor received us very kindly and gave us much good counsel on the subject of citizenship, giving us some instructions as to how we should live under the rule of the State if we should become the children of the same. He talked to us as though he was talking to his own son who had just come from a far country and asked his father's permission to stay in the household" (61).

As early as the eighteenth century, the Ojibwe adapted their trade organization to include economic relationships with the French and the English who settled in Michigan. Though antithetical to their understanding of the relationship between humanity and the land, they purchased land as soon as it was available to them, avoiding forced expulsion to a reservation. Melissa Pflug claims, "Shifts in traditional ethics were not signs of decline [in Ojibwe culture] but creative adjustments to new sociocultural situations" (41, 42). The Ojibwe understood identity to be relationship: "The actions that they called for in others were intended to confirm what 'I' and to 'you' and who 'we' are to 'them'" (39). The Ojibwe's adaptability is evident through the nineteenth-century acceptance of intermarriage in the region and the twenty-first-century survival of their native language and customs. Hemingway's exposure to this value system certainly informed his understanding that racial identity is negotiable. Petoskey residents, however, show less knowledge about their Native American neighbors.

An article in the *Petoskey News*, "Fight to Preserve Land to Papooses Who Are the Prey of 'Land Grafters,'" describes the success of Miss Kate Barnard in protecting the rights of Native American property owners. In addition to the use of the pejorative term "papooses," which was common at the time, the article reports on new legislation giving Barnard jurisdiction over her "Indian wards": "The law gives Miss Barnard jurisdiction over all Indian orphan minors whom, she said, had been the prey of 'Land Grafters' owing to their rich possessions in oil wells and farming land. She declared that her department has brought the sale of Indian children's land to a minimum and that this class of land grafting has practically ceased" (14 October 1915).

There is no evidence a Native American adult was consulted about or given power over these "Indian orphan minors." Instead, the support of the courts for Barnard's actions validate their social efficacy and reinforce whiteness as progressive, educated, and in charge of dispensing power and identity. Such social constructions were not questioned and reflect less a bias against Native Americans—which progressive white Americans were working to eliminate— than a lack of awareness about what was demanded of whiteness if the bias against others was to be truly eliminated.

Racism—both blatant and silent—was present in Oak Park and Petoskey, but it was tethered to a progressivism that complicated blind acceptance of such constructed hierarchy. Such complication allowed astute observers to begin to question white privilege and made those committed to white privilege resist even more strongly. This complex racial world Hemingway inhabited as a youth seems ever present in American culture. I push my students to begin to examine more fully their own racial education.

> Active Learning Project: Students are asked to collect ten cultural artifacts from a city they have some connection to but do not consider their hometown. This could be a vacation spot, a retreat, a summer camp, an ancestral home, etc. They are to create a second Artifact Annotated Bibliography and complete a five-hundred-word statement highlighting at least three pressures evident in their own racial education from this location and three pressures from their hometown.

In Our Time

Though my students have read two chapters and two stories in Hemingway's first collection of short stories, I now introduce the book as a whole and argue that the initial success of *In Our Time* demonstrates Hemingway's early mastery of scrutinizing whiteness. *In Our Time* contains two stories with Native American characters ("Indian Camp" and "The Doctor and the Doctor's Wife"), one story with an African American character ("The Battler"), and one chapter with African American characters (chapter 15). Beyond that, the breadth of racial and national variety in Hemingway's first collection is dramatic: Turks, Greeks, Italians, Austrians, Hungarians, Spaniards, Germans, Swiss, Mexicans, Belgians, English, and Irish all populate the pages of *In Our Time*, and each is carefully identified not by stereotype but by name, locale, skin color, and behaviors that reflect a relationship to established whiteness. Though every chapter and story in *In Our Time* presents whiteness as a flawed and negotiable social construct, for the purposes of this essay I will consider only the first two stories, the ones my students encounter as they begin to develop a racial lens.

"Indian Camp," the first story of *In Our Time*,[8] displays the rigidity with which whiteness has interacted with otherness. The perception that whiteness is superior is demonstrated by the Native Americans' service to Nick, his father, and Uncle George. Though Native Americans may consider rowing the white doctor ashore as common courtesy, it is clear Dr. Adams expects such treatment. He makes no effort to help with the rowing and does not thank anyone for the assistance. Additionally, Dr. Adams emphasizes this perceived hierarchy by dismissing the potentially distracting screams of the woman enduring a breech birth: "But her screams are not important. I don't hear them because they are not important" (*CSS* 68). This remark exposes an ugly truth: the cultural status of this white male physician effectively empowers him, as he chooses, to assist or ignore Native Americans and women. In contrast, the Ojibwe men react to the woman's screams: her husband turns from the doctor; an Indian male assisting the birth smiles when she bites George's arm; the remaining males scatter to lessen confusion. Though Dr. Adams's words serve a medical purpose, Hemingway's juxtaposition of them to the Native Americans' reaction emphasizes how words can reassert white privilege. When used to solidify the separation between whites and Native Americans, language stifles communication: in the story, the mother never learns "what had become of the baby or anything" and the father, unable to escape her screams or the doctor's dismissive remarks, kills himself (69). Understandably, the Indians do not row the white doctor home.

It is important to remember that young Nick has watched his father throughout his entire encounter with the Native Americans and from his father is learning how to be a successful white male. However, Hemingway makes it clear to readers that the lesson Nick learns about whiteness—that he is essentially different from Native Americans and therefore invincible, free to believe that "he will never die" (70)—is false and childish. The ideas Nick understands as defining whiteness are unsustainable.

"The Doctor and the Doctor's Wife" challenges both constructions of whiteness and constructions of otherness. Here, the Native American Dick Boulton comes to work for, not to seek help from, Nick's father. Boulton's persistent confrontation of his employer initiates Hemingway's interrogation of the label "Indian." Society considers Boulton "a half-breed and many of the farmers around the lake believed he was really a white man. He was very lazy but a great worker once he was started" (73). Hemingway is careful to construct Boulton's race as distinct from his work ethic—which race makes him lazy, which a good worker? Society, however, cannot resist linking them. Many choose to believe Boulton a white man because he consistently questions his limited position. To believe an Indian capable of and interested in questioning a subservient position would mean the Indian does not need the guidance or discipline of the white man; it would negate white privilege and demand whiteness be redefined.

In his encounter with the doctor, Boulton shows how language negotiates the race and position of both the speaker and the subject. Boulton arrives verbally confrontational: "Doc... that's a nice lot of timber you've stolen." Ducking the accusation, Dr. Adams names the logs "driftwood." Boulton pursues "stolen," washing the first log to protect the saw and to "see who it belongs to": the "White and McNally" Company. Boulton continues: "I don't care who you steal from. It is none of my business." Perhaps Boulton wants to humiliate the doctor, but his usurpation of the power to name or bestow identity is his greater offense, for naming is a function of language reserved for whites. Naming, just like deciding what is important enough to actually be heard, is a white privilege, and Dick has dared to rename not only the doctor's property but the doctor himself. Dick's acts of renaming clearly fluster the doctor, making him red in the face and leading him to threaten Dick: "If you call me Doc once again, I'll knock your eye teeth down your throat" (74).

Boulton's renaming is a threat to the doctor's identity in part because the doctor's identity is defined by history. When a Native American man confronts a white man about stolen property, he challenges the commonly held historical myth that whites "discovered" America. Although Hemingway's Native American is willing to work with the white man, he just wants the white man to admit he has stolen, to refine his language, his sense of who he really is: "You know they're stolen as well as I do. It don't make any difference to me" (74). However, a white man's admission to a Native American that material he had "found" really belonged to someone else and was therefore stolen would be tantamount to admitting that the historical power structure of white privilege could be rewritten. My students and I work through the remaining chapters and stories in *In Our Time* honing our racial lens and bridging possible historical readings with our own contemporary understanding of the racial markers in the text. The final project focuses on the last two questions of the course: What is the racial education being offered Americans today? What do Hemingway's stories, still widely read, offer to the current American conversation about race?

> Active Learning Project: The final project requires each student to write a 2,000 to 2,500 word analysis of the racial culture depicted in one piece from *In Our Time*. This analysis demands a close reading of the text that examines the interactions

between characters to better understand how whiteness and otherness is represented in Hemingway's writing. The goal of this analysis is to identity and explain ways Hemingway either reinforces available racial imagery of his day or challenges it. The final portion of this paper argues that this particular story is either less or more relevant to modern readers because of the racial constructions in it.

The long-term popularity of Hemingway's stories both with the public and the academy makes them an ideal vehicle for examining attitudes about race in America. Hemingway was a cultural icon, who produced stories for nearly half a century and earned the highest honors in his field; his influence on literature and American culture cannot be denied. If race is a defining construct for American identity—and I believe it is—then Hemingway's comment or lack of comment on it matters.

Notes

1. *Suburban Promised Land* by Stan West et al. provides a history of the black community in Oak Park, Illinois, from 1880 to1980. It showcases documents from the Historical Society of Oak Park and River Forest. Research in this essay was the result of a personal visit to the research center (https://www.oprfhistory.org/).

2. Review of *Oak Leaves* between 1899 and 1919 suggests active African American civic and church groups operated separately from similar white groups.

3. Hemingway returned to Walloon Lake for extended stays in 1919 after recovering from his war injuries and in 1922 to marry Hadley Richardson. He made only one more brief visit in his lifetime.

4. See *Historic Bay View Cottages: Bay View, Michigan 1875–1975*, published by the Bay View Library Board.

5. See Rieser 128–60 for a compelling and detailed account of white liberalism and Chautauqua.

6. Many programs, newspaper articles, and other advertisements from the Bay View Chautauqua series are housed in the Bay View Archives in Petoskey, Michigan.

7. James L Morrice, treasurer of Emmet County; C. F. Newkirk, principal of Harbor Springs Public Schools; Charles R. Wright, ex-president, Harbor Springs; Charles W. Ingalls, notary public for Emmet County; Albert Hathaway, county clerk of Emmet County; William H. Lee, probate clerk and abstractor of titles; Arch. D. Metz, deputy register of deeds; Willard P. Gibson, pastor of the Presbyterian Church; and William H. Miller recommended Blackbird's work as "interesting and reliable" (4).

8. Upon acquiring the publishing rights to *In Our Time* from Boni & Liveright, Maxwell Perkins of Scribner asked Hemingway to write an introduction for the book's republication in 1930. Hemingway responded by submitting a short story, eventually titled "On the Quai at Smyrna," which became the first story of the edition. Edmund Wilson wrote an introduction to the story cycle that was published only with this edition.

Hemingway's Experts

Teaching Race in *Death in the Afternoon* and *Green Hills of Africa*

Ross K. Tangedal

> "The style is perfect, the execution is cynical."
> —Ernest Hemingway, *Death in the Afternoon*

> "M'Cola was not jealous of Droopy. He simply knew that Droop was a better man than he was. More of a hunter, a faster and a cleaner tracker, and a great stylist in everything he did."
> —Ernest Hemingway, *Green Hills of Africa*

Ernest Hemingway published two essential pieces of American nonfiction in the 1930s. *Death in the Afternoon* (1932) is a treatise on writing, authorship, and culture masked as a guide to Spanish bullfighting, while *Green Hills of Africa* (1935) is a complex exercise in narrative and memory presented as an African safari memoir. Of all of Hemingway's texts, none are more misunderstood, misread, underanalyzed, and undervalued than these two books. Save for a handful of short stories—including the oft-anthologized "The Short Happy Life of Francis Macomber" and "The Snows of Kilimanjaro" and the posthumously released *True at First Light* and *Under Kilimanjaro*—our understanding of Hemingway's relationship to Africa is based almost solely on his treatment of the continent and its inhabitants in *Green Hills of Africa*. Somewhat opposite is the breadth of his Hispanic-influenced texts. In novels (*The Sun Also Rises*, *For Whom the Bell Tolls*, *The Old Man and the Sea*), short stories ("The Undefeated," "The Capital of the World"), and nonfiction (*Death in the Afternoon*, *The Dangerous Summer*),

Hemingway addresses Hispanic traditions and rituals while commenting on various ethnographic standards. Scholarly collections have been constructed as reading companions for both texts under the direction of Miriam Mandel, and various scholars (including Mandel, Thomas Strychacz, Barbara Lounsberry, Marc Dudley, Hilary K. Justice, Nancy Bredendick, Robert W. Trogdon, Ryan Hediger, Lisa Tyler, Kevin Maier, and Emily Wittman) have clearly elevated the importance of these texts in a variety of contexts. However, both texts contain fascinating moments of racial and cultural realization, complexity, aversion, immersion, and consumption, which are little discussed in Hemingway scholarship. Though a significant faction of scholarship on Hemingway and his treatment of race has entered the critical canon (including works by Gary Holcomb, Amy Strong, and Marc Dudley), the two texts I examine still suffer from a lack of scholarly attention when it comes to race. In this essay I will present a teaching approach for Hemingway's complex nonfiction texts with a critical eye toward the complication of race.

In specific textual (and visual) situations, Hemingway uses matador Juan Belmonte, picador Zurito (*Death in the Afternoon*), and hunting guides Droopy and M'Cola (*Green Hills of Africa*) for a variety of purposes, most notably to showcase the strength and expertise he expects bullfighters and trackers to exhibit. These "experts" are complicated agents of Hemingway's narratives, and in my estimation he carefully erases his experts' identities in favor of his own representations. Several key questions of race always arise when approaching Belmonte, the Zuritos, Droopy, and M'Cola: do their ethnic identities disappear throughout Hemingway's texts and leave us with an idealized bullfighter and two idealized hunters rather than flesh-and-blood individuals? What role do their ethnicities play in this disappearance? Does Hemingway intend for these men to transcend racial difference in favor of form and art? Or is it a calculated removal because Hemingway's *aficionado* status requires the likening of fighters and hunters to objectified forms rather than humans (with differing races and ethnic identities)? These questions always garner discussions and papers that center on various interpretations of fetishisms, objectification, racial indifference, ethnic standardization, and the effects of art. Hemingway's use of Belmonte, the Zuritos, Droopy, and M'Cola provides insight into the racial standards he both recognized and neglected. Though each of their textual positions are minor compared to Hemingway's, their aesthetic and pedagogical impact are a major component in understanding the fine racial line the author rode in developing his nonfiction texts. Teaching these developments to students shows Hemingway's artistic dexterity and his attention to racial detail.

Students understand the racial divide Hemingway requires us to ride in order to understand bullfighting and big-game hunting, and eventually race disappears in favor of action, motion, and expertise. Whether this disappearance is acceptable (and commended) or detestable (and rejected), students react strongly when confronted with the structural and aesthetic representations of Belmonte, the Zuritos, Droopy, and M'Cola. Hemingway's complex depiction of race in his "experts" represents the new attention scholarship and pedagogy must recognize in order to develop a more fully realized and racially relevant Hemingway classroom experience.

Death in the Afternoon (1932)

As the American *aficionado*, Hemingway positioned himself in a dominant pedagogical and critical role by choosing the Spanish bullfight as a means of artistic and cultural conveyance in his landmark 1932 text *Death in the Afternoon*. Hemingway makes clear the endeavor to show both his knowledge of the tradition itself and his understanding of the participants involved. Not only does he utilize significant historical bullfighters as guideposts for his study, but he directs the reception of specific Spanish traits (*pundonor,* or honor) and processes (*suertes,* or bullfighting maneuvers). His direction, both aesthetically and structurally, complicates the relationship between the American Hemingway and the Hispanic bullfighting culture. This complication yields significant pedagogical and analytical benefit, both for scholars and teachers of Hemingway's work. Using bullfighting as an entry point, I argue that Hemingway, in a prime authoritative position, deliberately casts bullfighters Belmonte, Old Zurito, and Young Zurito as opposites in *Death in the Afternoon,* playing with art and race in a highly original manner. Not only can the reading of Belmonte and the Zuritos complicate Hemingway's racial contexts, but this reading can also highlight his creative consumption of those contexts. Belmonte's background is absent aside from his role as the great matador, while the Zuritos earn subtle individual mentions based on grit and true honor. In both instances, Hemingway complicates racial identification in the three men, leading students to question his intentions and consider his claims on the sport.

At first glance, Hemingway's treatment of bullfighters is not unlike his treatment of other parts of the bullfight. Much like bulls, spectators, and even the sun, Hemingway considers the bullfighters part of a larger whole, for "the aficionado, or lover of the bullfight, may be said, broadly then, to be one who has this sense of the tragedy and ritual of the fight so that the minor aspects are not important except as they relate to the whole" (*DIA* 9). His extended discussion on bullfighters takes place during his lengthy dialogue between "Author" and Old Lady," in which he differentiates between several matadors, including Juan Belmonte, Joselito, Chicuelo, Maera, Niño de la Palma, Manuel Granero, and Marcial Lalanda. Names are important to Hemingway, just as the names of countries, towns, and villages are important. He sees these names as placeholders of specific expectations. For instance, Belmonte was the *de facto* father of modern bullfighting, and "once he had done it all bullfighters had to do it, or attempt to do it since there is no going back in the matter of sensations." Joselito is presented as the inheritor of Belmonte's technique, though Hemingway instructs readers of Joselito's superior athleticism, talent, grace, and knowledge of bulls. Regardless of this superiority, Belmonte's "way of working" set the standard by which all fighters must adhere, since "he did not accept any rules made without testing whether they might be broken, and he was a genius and an artist. The way Belmonte worked was not a heritage, nor a development; it was a revolution." The competition between the two sparked what Hemingway refers to as "a golden age in spite of the fact that it was in the process of being destroyed." I impress this upon students to show Hemingway's close scrutiny of the fighters' actions and how a spectator (which Hemingway ultimately is) can find fault in even the best of matadors. Though subtle, his criticism of Belmonte and Joselito rests on their revolution and destruction of the sport wrought by their technique. Belmonte invented technique from necessity (due to his body type) and Joselito successfully translated that technique with his own genius. This proved successful in the ring, and spectators expected the "decadent," "impossible," and "almost depraved" technique, which led to the breeding down of bulls in order to assure the genius in the ring. Eventually "bullfighting was left with the new decadent method, the almost impossible technique, the bred down bulls and, as bullfighters, only the bad ones, the hardy, tough ones who had not been able to learn the new method and so no longer pleased" (69, 70). No mention is necessarily given of the men as humans, but rather as forces upon a sport. The mythic stature of both fighters is similar to sports fans' tendencies to deify athletes in action but refuse to recognize their human qualities. Students relate to this comparison, and from here discussions on racial identity can take place.

I ask students what role these fighters' ethnic backgrounds play in their characterization and whether or not Hemingway pays tribute to those backgrounds. Belmonte first appears as a qualifier to a definition of matadors: "the best of all are the cynical ones when they are still devout; or after; when having been devout, then cynical, they become devout again by cynicism. Juan Belmonte is an example of the last stage" (59). This appearance sets up the treatment of bullfighters throughout the text. Like Belmonte, few of the fighters are seen as anything but bullfighters; they are essentially art forms amid the tapestry of the sport. Each fighter represents a specific quality or movement in the tradition, but Hemingway deviates slightly from this method when dealing with Manuel and Antonio de la Haba (both named Zurito). Though mentioned in passing earlier, the two fighters are given backstories in chapter nineteen. Young Zurito has a home ("he was from Cordoba"), distinguishing facial markers ("dark and rather thin; his face very sad in repose; serious and with a deep sense of honor"), and a detailed fighting history (254, 256). He and his father were both inspirations for Hemingway's earlier short story "The Undefeated," since Young Zurito possessed great skill (like Belmonte) but bad luck. Hemingway recounts how Zurito would be bumped and faint while killing, though he killed "all of his forty-two bulls" (257). The public disliked his fainting, and Hemingway concludes: "So that season, in which he gave the most harrowing display of courage I have ever seen, did him no good," for "too much honor destroys a man quicker than too much of any other fine quality and with a little bad luck it ruined Zurito in one season" (257–58). There is no doubting the similarities between young Zurito here and the character of Manuel Garcia in "The Undefeated," and a further link rests on the depiction of Old Zurito in Hemingway's photo-essay following the text of *Death in the Afternoon*. Just as the picador Zurito in "The Undefeated" shows grace and wisdom through action, the real-life Zurito possesses the same qualities while pic-ing a bull.

Hemingway's first photo of a bullfighter shows Old Zurito in the process of pic-ing a "cowardly" bull (285). The photo shows numerous spectators, suspended by the pic, but Hemingway immediately creates competing dualisms between man and art, and man and beast. Hemingway's caption begins: "Zurito, from Cordoba, one of the greatest picadors who ever lived, shooting the stick a little back of where it should go, having let the bull get the horn in so he may be well pegged. The style is perfect, the execution is cynical, and the horse, who will be dead very shortly . . . is not panicky because those knees have convinced him that he is being properly ridden" (285). The pic-ing of the bull is key to preparing the bull for the matador, yet Hemingway is critical (both in the text and with his choice of photography) of the picador's ultimate role in the corrida. Even though the matador, "takes the responsibility and runs the greatest danger of death," and therefore makes more money, Hemingway argues that "good picadors . . . are ridiculously underpaid if the matador is receiving ten thousand pesatas and over. If they are not good at their trade they are a definite liability to the matador" (201). They are reduced to what Hemingway calls "day laborers compared to the matadors," but "in spite of how badly paid a profession it is these men keep on, living always close to hunger, from the illusion that they may make a living from the bulls and from the pride of being fighters" (201–2). The ultimate pride is the knowledge that a kill is imminent, and the picador's role in that kill essentializes him, though he is underrepresented socially and financially.

It would obviously please Hemingway, then, to present a picador (Zurito being one of the best, as he sees it) as the first human subject in his photo-essay—a man fighting with dexterity and imperfection in order to achieve a perfect result. Hemingway points out the problems with Zurito's pic. The stick is "a little back of where it should go," and Zurito has thrown his hat to provoke the bull's charge, something Hemingway chastises other fighters for. However, this photo concerns the justification of Zurito's actions, whether they are correct or not. The caption (as quoted above) relies on dualism. One, Zurito is not a matador, and the reader therefore will have a lesser reaction to the picador. Naturally, the matador has more "responsibility," and his presentation is more pure and true to the kill itself (since he does the killing), but our introduction to the fighting men (to go with the fighting bulls) rests on the subordinated Zurito's great shoulders and his "perfect" and "cynical" pic (201, 285). Students see the dualism between art and adjustment in both sporting and writing terms. However, what complicates these representations is the lack of attention Hemingway gives to the bullfighters' identities outside of the ring, where their ethnic identities and personalities would certainly show through.

By the end of the book, students wonder whether the author considers his role as the great white teacher and observer among the Spanish people. The term *white gaze* takes on new meaning when viewing Hemingway's photo-essay, as he directs the reader/viewer through careful captioning and textual placement. In short, does it matter that Belmonte and the Zuritos are people? Is it their forms that readers (especially of the time) will need to grapple with in order to understand the tradition, or will readers require a more fully formed human presence to balance the violent and inevitable conclusion of any bullfight? Thomas Strychacz notes that "*Death in the Afternoon* is as much a compendium of forms of spectating as it is of forms of bullfighting" (160), and "the reader's role at the arena of writing matches the equivocal role of the bullfighter's audience, which does not perform, but whose presence is nonetheless constitutive of the performance" (162). Hemingway knew going in to his experiment that readers would know little to nothing about Spain and its people and even less about bullfighting. Early on during research, Hemingway wrote editor Maxwell Perkins that the book he wanted to write would be "a long one to write because it is not to be just a history and text book or apologia for bull fighting—but instead, if possible, bull fighting its-self" (Bruccoli 53). By presenting each of his bullfighters in certain lights, Hemingway forces readers to react, even if they know nothing about the process. We come to admire the Zuritos, especially the younger, though we are conflicted about Belmonte and others. We recognize skill, talent, honor, grace, and intellect, but not race. However, as we see more exclusively with *Green Hills of Africa*, an important idea is whether Hemingway indeed recognizes race by essentializing his experts' actions and talents rather than their race. Is he, as Marc Dudley argues, "razing the color line" (7)? With *Green Hills of Africa*, Hemingway pushes his experimentation further, and forces students into a state of flux regarding identity, action, and imperialism.

Green Hills of Africa (1935)

Green Hills of Africa is significant for a number of reasons. Hemingway seamlessly blurs time to create a nonlinear narrative centered on landscape, atmosphere, and "word pictures" (Reynolds, *1930s* 20); he counteracts the nonfictional elements of the safari with the prose style of a novel, particularly in a single-sentence, stream-of-consciousness description of the Gulf Stream and artistic longevity (*GHOA* 148–50); he analyzes the role of critics in American letters and cites their negative practice of forcing writers to "write masterpieces," as opposed to taking risks (*GHOA* 24); and finally, the work tests Hemingway's notion of the "fourth and fifth dimension in writing," whereby time and memory fuse with the concrete realities of the landscape and the hunt (27). *Green Hills of Africa*—like *Death in the Afternoon*—is as much about writing and authorship as it is about the natural world, and as Hemingway wrote Perkins on 30 April 1934, "My idea of a career is never to write a phony line, never fake, never cheat, never be sucked in by the y.m.c.a. movement of the moment, and to give them as much literature in a book as any son of a bitch has ever gotten in the same number of words" (Bruccoli 208). In his book on hunting in Africa, Hemingway performs for his readers, his critics, and himself. Strychacz refers to the book as a "drama of manhood-fashioning acted out before an audience that crucially affects his sense of manhood by approving or scorning his efforts" (171). Similarly, Kevin Maier discusses a dichotomy inherent in Hemingway's hunting ideology, asking "How could the hunter be at once an elite individual and a democratic everyman? How could the hunter be both a gentleman sportsman and a frontier backwoodsman?" (267). Robert O. Stephens clarifies Hemingway's awareness "of the pitfalls of the travel-writing tradition. Hemingway thought he could practice it more honestly than some" (65). Robert W. Trogdon describes the work as Hemingway's "most involved and systematic answer to his critics" (2), and Michael Reynolds points to early criticism of the book, where "no one saw clearly what he was trying for in his multi-dimensional prose, but if he did it well enough, no one on first reading should have noticed" (*1930s* 215). In many ways, the book was a complex dual experiment for Hemingway. He wanted to be both critically accepted and dismissive of criticism; he wanted readers to track kudu with him and get lost in the African savannah; he wanted to write the action and emotion of a novel without writing a novel; but even more intriguing, Hemingway wanted to explain the ritual manhood of his guides (as he did with matadors in *Death in the Afternoon*), by complicating their identities and presenting them somewhere between people and hunting bodies.

Marc Dudley notes that in *Green Hills of Africa* Hemingway "vacillates between embracing Africa's countrymen as kindred spirits and surveying the country as Occidental tourist; to be sure, his surveillance time in this narrative far outweighs that spent in active embrace" (21). My students and I discuss imperialism and colonization, especially in regards to the complicated sociopolitical history of Africa, and that discussion leads into Hemingway's first description of Droopy, which begins chapter three: "Droopy was a real savage with lids to his eyes that nearly covered them, handsome, with a great deal of style, a fine hunter and a beautiful tracker. He was about thirty-five, I should think, and wore only a piece of cloth, knotted over one shoulder, and a fez that some tracker had given him." In line with Dudley's discussion of vacillation, Droopy is at first a "savage," the form a stranger may see him as, and certainly in line with imperialist ideology. As the description continues, Hemingway modifies the savage stereotype by emphasizing his talents rather than his appearance, ultimately seeing Droopy as both savage (the loincloth) and modern (the fez). On the contrary, he describes M'Cola as wearing "an old U.S. Army khaki tunic, complete with buttons," and "a pair of shorts, his fuzzy wool curler's cap, and a knitted army sweater we wore when washing the tunic." Hemingway sees the hunters as contraries, though they both possess valuable and honest skills. The elder tracker, M'Cola, "ceased being an old timer and we were hunting together; he and I hunting together and Droopy in command of the show" (*GHOA* 46–47). As with his bullfighters, Hemingway does away with individualism in favor of their becoming part of something greater, something more complete. At crucial points Hemingway uses his guides to introduce two critical components of hunting—durability and brotherhood—and these moments allow students to critically examine the author's use of real people to underscore the ethereal qualities of the hunt.

During the flashback in Part II, Hemingway compares scars with Droopy, for "my own scars were all informal, some irregular and sprawling, others simply puffy welts. I had one on my forehead that people still commented on, asking if I had bumped my head; but Droop had handsome ones beside his cheekbones and others, symmetrical and decorative, on his chest and belly" (*GHOA* 53). Similarly, Hemingway wrote Perkins two years earlier and commented openly on critics and their role in his public authority: "I'm just getting to the age when a novelist really starts—And they all (critics) have tried to bury me after every book. Instead of being brittle am very durable (in spite of G. Stein) and only bones I've ever broken were broken by the full weight of a car turning over on my arm and by high explosive" (Bruccoli 199–200). At play are Hemingway's textual and actual wounds. His "informal" wounding does not compare to the tribal wounds he admires in Droopy and others, but his durability and acceptance matters in terms of action, writing, and hunting. After shooting a reedbuck and bleeding the animal out, he starts "to open him, with the little knife, still showing off to Droopy, and emptying him neatly took out the liver, cut away the gall, and laying the liver on a hummock, put the kidneys aside" (*GHOA* 54). The showing off is a result of Hemingway's subtle reaction to Droopy's superior scarring, as he enacts something visceral to counteract what we perceive he lacks. Strychacz argues that "performance in *Green Hills* always involves an unsettling negotiation between the primary meanings of the word: performance as an unfolding in action of one's will, and performance as confronting one's actions to an audience's expectations" (173). Between personal will and exterior expectation, Hemingway accepts Droopy's hunting acumen, as well as his "good tricks," which leads to increased personal confidence: "I knew that I was shooting well and I had that feeling of well being and confidence that is so much more pleasant to have than to hear about" (*GHOA* 55). However, in defining his own experience Hemingway denies his readers' access, as he prefers to own his feelings rather than relay them to others. Hemingway complicates his own textual play by bringing his readers in and out of the experience; this effectively forces readers to "compete" with Hemingway's imagination.

Much later in the narrative, and out of the flashback, Hemingway and M'Cola come upon the Masai village, full of people who were "the tallest, best-built, handsomest people I had ever seen and first truly light-hearted people I had seen in Africa." M'Cola tells Hemingway that the villagers are "*Good* Masai," before the author moves into a lengthy explanation of brotherhood: "They had that attitude that makes brothers, that unexpressed but instant and complete acceptance that you must be Masai wherever it is you come from. That attitude you only get from the best of the English, the best of the Hungarians and the very best Spaniards; the thing that used to be the most clear distinction of nobility when there was nobility" (*GHOA* 221). I point students to Hemingway's treatment of *afición* in *The Sun Also Rises* when Jake discusses bullfighting with Montoya, who "always smiled as if bullfighting were a very deep secret between the two of us: a rather shocking but really very deep secret that we knew about" (136). Then students are brought back to *Death in the Afternoon*, in many ways a book-length example of Hemingway's *afición*. Drawing the narrative of secret brotherhood between the texts helps students see the premium Hemingway put on being part of ritual activities, secret languages, and detailed knowledge bases. In the final third of *Green Hills of Africa*, Hemingway describes the action of speaking between hunters, bringing together the notion of durability (first seen with Droopy's wounds) and brotherhood (represented by M'Cola and the Masai). After a short description, Hemingway explains his actions: "You ask how this was discussed, worked out, and understood with the bar of language, and I say it was as freely discussed and clearly understood as though we were a cavalry patrol all speaking the same language. We were all hunters . . . and the whole thing could be worked out, understood, and agreed to without using anything but a forefinger to signal and a hand to caution" (*GHOA* 251). Just as Montoya signals his brotherhood with Jake by touching his shoulder in *The Sun Also Rises* (136), Hemingway's guides represent both durability—only seasoned hunters would understand the meaning of the silent motions—and brotherhood.

At this point students find themselves admiring both Droopy and M'Cola for the reasons mentioned above, and this is no surprise. In *Death in the Afternoon* the Zuritos gained students' admiration because Hemingway packaged them that way, and in *Green Hills of Africa* we are meant to read his two main guides as hard working, intelligent, and essential to the goal of the hunts. But this causes issues, once again, due to Hemingway's oftentimes derisive descriptions of M'Cola "tracking slowly, steadily, and absolutely absorbed in the problem. His bare, bald head gleamed with sweat and when it ran down in his eyes he would pluck a grass stem, hold it with his hand and shave the sweat off his forehead and bald black crown with the stem" (*GHOA* 268–69). Dudley notes that Hemingway's narrative "actively and completely divorces M'Cola of history, an act whose import cannot be overstated," and the book itself is "a celebration of the imperial ideal and an underscoring of the color line. Within its scope, the land, the animals, the people that are Africa—all fall prey to the white man's gaze" (124, 126–27). Both *Death in the Afternoon* and *Green Hills of Africa* are products of whiteness, Hemingway seeing landscapes and people as parts of larger ritual structures meant to either confirm or deny acceptance into a certain act. But even more complicated, the two books seek to establish Hemingway's writing experimentation, whereby large portions of each narrative feature composites of the author, but not the writer himself. If race is to be understood in either work, attention must be given to Hemingway's treatment of his experts and their activities, for through them the purpose of bullfighting and hunting lives and breathes, whether we agree with it or not.

Conclusions

In the final chapter of *Death in the Afternoon*, Hemingway implies that his book alone wasn't enough, that "if I could have made this enough of a book it would have had everything in it" (270). Similarly, near the end of *Green Hills of Africa*, he insists that "a country was made to be as we found it. We are the intruders and after we are dead we may have ruined it but it will still be there and we don't know what the next changes are" (284–285). Ever cognizant of his role as a foreigner in Spain and an intruder in Africa, Hemingway reminds readers that even he is incapable of rendering truthfully all that each has to offer. Therefore, teaching *Death in the Afternoon* or *Green Hills of Africa* is an extremely difficult task. Not only is the subject matter difficult (especially in the former), and the narrative experimentation disorienting (i.e., the flashback in *GHOA*), but Hemingway toys with his readers to the point of frustration in both cases. I always begin by teaching students *In Our Time* prior to either book. Through these stories, students are made aware of style, technique, and confidence, elements that he expanded upon in his nonfiction books. I offer several critical pieces during reading for students to use as context, including Dudley's chapter on *Green Hills of Africa* in *Hemingway, Race, and Art*; Hilary Justice's chapter on *Death in the Afternoon* in *The Bones of the Others*; Strychacz's chapters on *Death in the Afternoon* and *Green Hills of Africa* in *Hemingway's Theaters of Masculinity*; and Robert Trogdon's chapters on the composition and publication of both books in *The Lousy Racket*. From these contexts, the class begins asking major questions of authenticity. How seriously are we to take Hemingway during his "wanderlust" (Dudley 126) in Africa or his sojourn in Spain? How much can readers personally bring to either text in order to read confidently?

I ask a lot of my students when assigning these texts, for in them we are made aware of Ernest Hemingway's authorial character, his contentious relationship with his own celebrity, and the inner workings of literary publication from manuscript to post-publication criticism. Race factors in to my teaching as a natural result of Hemingway's characterizations. Once students get their hands on the photo-essay in *DIA*, a new understanding encompasses the room. Why is Old Zurito, mentioned briefly in text, the first bullfighter we see following photos of bulls? It is an imperfect photo showcasing an imperfect bull being pic-ed—a prelude to the great action. Zurito's intense and determined facial expression outweighs the faces of nearly every other matador in photos to come. Their calm, performing faces seem somewhat odd next to Zurito's ferocity (*DIA* 284–85). Similarly, what is Hemingway's obsession with Droopy's lack of clothing and M'Cola's unique, borrowed wardrobe? Is he contrasting elements of imperialism with notions of independence? Students seek to answer these questions and others when confronted with two of Hemingway's most challenging works, and by focusing on race alongside narrative technique, the resulting projects and discussions form a fascinating summation of Hemingway's experimentation.

Teaching race in Hemingway can only bring about more avenues of analysis, greater realizations, and stronger connections between author and subject matter. If we are prepared to begin teaching the racial complexities inherent in Hemingway's fiction, we should be brave enough to begin teaching the racial complications of his nonfiction experiments. When Hemingway pressed to do something different, he usually found criticism, and hopefully time has rectified the critical misreading and omission of *Death in the Afternoon* and *Green Hills of Africa* in literature classrooms. Contextualizing race in both texts primes students for serious discussions of authority, power, authenticity, and narrative purpose, and with a little help from Hemingway's "experts," the texts become more valuable to teachers and students alike.

Racial Politics to Social Action
Teaching Self/Other Dilemma in Hemingway's Works

Mayuri Deka

Political scientist Robert D. Putnam, in his book *Bowling Alone,* revealed his astonishing research findings that people living in highly diverse communities in comparison to those living in low diversity communities seem to mistrust both their in-group and their out-group more. This lack of trust corresponds to less civic and political involvement evident in diminishing confidence in local government, less belief in a personal ability to affect the political process, fewer citizens registering to vote, and a reduction in charity and volunteering. Putnam admits that in the long-run successful communities create new forms of social solidarity and more encompassing identities, while in the short run, "the features of social organization such as networks, norms, and social trust that facilitate coordination and cooperation for mutual benefit" are declining with increasing immigration and racial diversity (67). Putnam calls this "social capital"—a reality for most of our students. Therefore, these findings become even more pertinent in teaching Ernest Hemingway within our classrooms.

Hemingway's attempt to create a certain timelessness sets down, as Carlos Baker points out, "things-in-motion" (*Writer as Artist* 62) within a certain flexible framework. Hemingway endeavors to exert rigorous linguistic order over an emotional, chaotic world, crystallizing the disillusionment of the World War I generation and trying to make sense of a world turned upside down in texts like *A Moveable Feast* and *A Farewell to Arms*. Hemingway presents a society that is disintegrating by creating a framework of constant moral fluidity and bringing into question our own underlying belief system. Characters in Hemingway's works represent the dilemma of the set of people who are all negatively affected by society's disintegration, either physically, emotionally, psychologically, or morally. His life and works reflect a similar struggle to establish a secure identity; while identifying with Other cultures by imagining himself in an insider space he, nonetheless, always returned to his homeland.

Teaching this hyphenated reality must include complex identity formations. The philosophical terms *Self* and *Other* refer to the interdependent relationship between Hemingway's and the students' identities to the target race/culture. In Lacanian terms, the Self is defined through a continuous exposure to otherness so that it shapes itself in the Other's image or in opposition to it. The negotiation with the Other is seen in our students' dilemma of creating a secure identity in a diaspora and in Hemingway's relation to America and the other cultures he experienced.[1] While an insecure identity leads to bias and prejudice, Hemingway crafts a polyvocal immigrant tradition by identifying with multiple cultures/races.

The complex negotiation between the Self and Other that is evident in Hemingway's relation to America and his other adopted cultures is particularly suited not only to learning about language and culture but also to enhancing students' prosocial behavior. This can be achieved by supporting and securing their identity development and by increasing their capacity for empathy through the reading of racial politics in his texts. The pedagogical strategies suggested in this article facilitate the development of students' complex identity contents (such as race, class, gender, sexuality, and so on) to make them more open to identifying commonalities between the Self and Other based on universal affective states and life conditions, while taking practical steps to alleviate the Other's suffering and engage in social change. This is done by reading Hemingway's works through the complex framework of Self/Other racial politics.

Background and Objectives

In the last three decades, scholars have attempted to develop a coherent framework for transforming dominant paradigms into decentered, pedagogical strategies. The general belief about these reformulations within academia has been that the greater the exposure to texts and the more time spent with the Other, then the deeper is the understanding of a race/culture generally seen as distant. The result of this rethinking is seen in the diversity of Hemingway's works being included in syllabi and the contexts within which these texts are being interpreted and taught. These revisionist approaches stretch from the postmodernist and post-structuralist stances to the activist voices previously silenced—the gendered, class, cultural, and racial minorities. One example of this is seen in Judith Fetterley's "resisting reader," who reevaluates male-centered works from the formerly marginalized woman's perspective. It was hoped that these approaches would lead to a sense of identification and unity within the student body, expanding eventually to the community at large.

The response to this belief has been the "standard story" that Gerald Graff describes in *Beyond the Culture Wars*, "which implies that the business of teaching literature is basically simple: Just put the student in front of a good book, provide teachers who are encouraging and helpful, and the rest presumably will take care of itself" (72). While this is a valid course of action, it is becoming increasingly evident that there is growing cognitive dissonance and disengagement of students in literature classrooms and in the sociopolitical trends. Exposure to diversity and desegregation are not resulting in the expected and avowed solidarity and understanding within communities. Instead of becoming more unified, the opposite is happening—social well-being and social capital are lowering, and individuals in diverse communities are "hunkering down" to protect their economic and social privileges, which they fear they will lose to minorities. Therefore, an alternative strategy is needed for a greater understanding of Hemingway's works that further sustains a secure identity in the students and results in empathy and prosocial behavior.

What Is a Secure Empathic Identity?

The more students care about something, the more interest they will have in learning about it and taking action that results in prosocial change. The recent reformulations in pedagogical strategies have mostly been centered on increasing the student's interest base in the content of the texts read in the classroom. Educators put a concerted effort in making the texts appealing to the students. Within Hemingway studies, this can be seen in the diverse multimodal and minority perspectives used to interpret his life and works with concentrations on social interpretations. However, students must learn not only how to engage in new kinds of intellectual and social actions by incorporating diverse realms of their life but also how to understand the personal and social implications of their knowledge. When students learn something about themselves or about Others, such an experience generates a new self-image along with a vision of what they want to become through relations with Others.

Moreover, research by William Damon shows that people are more disposed to help another person if they can empathize with them and identify commonalities between the Self and Other. These similarities are based on universal affective states (like contentment, despondency) and life conditions (like birth, death). However, an openness to finding commonalities with the racial/cultural Other requires a Self who is secure in itself. As Mark Bracher discussed in *Radical Pedagogy*, a secure identity is characterized by certain qualities, including continuity, consistency, agency, distinction, belonging, and meaning. These have to be present in a person before they can engage empathically with new information. While some of the qualities are concerned with the intrapersonal process of maintaining a sense of Self, the rest are enacted in the relationship of the Self with the Other. Bracher defines these terms to encapsulate both the inter- and intrapersonal interactions that the Self engages in while defining itself. *Consistency* is the enactment of specific identity components that creates a sense of oneself as a unique being different from the Other. *Continuity* defines the emotional and psychological persistence of an identity over time. This is closely connected to *distinction*, which defines the Self as separate from the Other. However, the Self also defines itself based on the impact it has on the Other. *Belonging* is the experience of that effect on otherness, which provides the Self with evidence that it exists. Similarly, *agency* is the ability to enact action, which creates meaning in the world. Finally, *meaning* is the sense of mattering in the world and is based on the feedback from the Other. The presence of these characteristics defines a secure sense of Self, and an identity-supporting pedagogy must provide recognition for these qualities. This is especially pertinent not only in understanding the complexity of Hemingway's race relations but also in bringing about lasting change and including more empathic characteristics in student identity.

Empathy is defined here as the ability to take the space of the Other and occupy affective states more appropriate to another's situation than the Self's. The ability in human beings to imagine oneself in another's place and the power of these represented events are so strong that one need only to imagine the Other's pain to feel empathic distress. Research by Daniel Batson et al. shows how reading a note or listening to a radio interview results in the participants feeling empathic distress for the people they read about or listened to and taking steps to help the victim.[2] However, this process of identification is only possible in our students if through reading Hemingway's works the Self is secure in its identity as a consistent, meaningful being that matters.

The Role of Literature

Literature, especially fiction, is something not real, something perhaps made up. Therefore, as Keith Oatley points out "[f]iction has come to mean falsehood" (101). This suspicion of fiction, however, negates the seminal role that it plays in simulating coherent forms of truth and gives students insight into their own sense of Self as well as the Other. Larsen and Seilman stressed the importance of reading fiction, which results in remembered memories in the reader. This process of remembering, which generates meaning for the reader, is based in the personal resonance with the reader's life, which is connected to the themes of the story. For instance, students tend to identify with the love story in *A Farewell to Arms* as they draw connections with their own life experiences. Oatley concludes that "[i]t seems likely that the provenance of fiction is the ordinary conversation. . . . Such conversation is most frequently about what people have done, what they are up to, and what the personal implications of such doings might be" (109). Thus, while nonfiction is seen as representative of real life, fiction also reflects reality.

Hild Hoff emphasizes that it is because of this close relationship between fiction and reality that "'the learners' own prejudices and fixed opinions about other societies may be challenged as they interact with the text on a personal level" (31). This would enhance the reader's personal engagement with the works. In nonfiction, like Hemingway's *A Moveable Feast*, this engagement is easier to achieve, as the elements of disbelief and suspicion are usually not present. Students are more willing to accept the world as presented in the work rather than dismissing it as a figment of the author's imagination. Claire Kramsch points out that the role of the teacher is, therefore, to help students see the connections in the texts to their own lives (44). Achieving this expands the student's worldview by reducing their bias toward the Other and increasing what Peter Singer calls "the expanding circle" of empathy (101). While the inner circle includes family and friends, the circle widens with increased knowledge and understanding to embrace more of the Other. However, this process is dependent on the secure identity of the Self, and the role of the teacher becomes to include diverse knowledge beyond the limited domain of the student's inner world.

Encounters with Race/Culture while Reading Hemingway

Hemingway has dominated the American consciousness in a singular fashion. Carl P. Eby unequivocally states, "[I]n the popular imagination, Ernest the monovocally masculine bullfight aficionado, boxer, hunter, deep-sea fisherman, and pitchman for Ballantine Ale and khaki pants still looms over the American literary horizon like a testosterone-crazed colossus" (3). The image of Hemingway as a macho, alcohol-guzzling, big-game-hunting womanizer has deeply penetrated both the popular culture and the academic departments in the last half century. Movies like *Hemingway and Gellhorn* have also added to the increasing repertoire of studies on Hemingway. However, most of these considerations on Hemingway have traditionally projected him with a unique identity—especially one as occupying an essential racial/cultural space.

Though the logocentric attitude toward Hemingway had suffered a setback in the last couple decades in the hands of some feminists, the complex racial relationships in his works have yet to be fully analyzed.[3] Hemingway's texts, like *A Moveable Feast* and *A Farewell to Arms,* provide a crucial insight into the conflict that Hemingway underwent in establishing a secure identity. Nostalgic about the Michigan of his early years and mourning the loss of the preindustrial, natural society, which reflected the basic, most admirable tenets of American culture, Hemingway struggled against a fast-changing world. In discussing the role of the Jew (as representative of all immigrants) in *The Sun Also Rises,* Gay Wilentz states, "Although Hemingway does not articulate the values of the pre-industrial time, it is clear what he doesn't want—an alien population who could succeed without any of the breeding, manliness, and finesse of Anglo-America" (192). The seminal role that American values played in Hemingway's conception of the ideal society and the characteristics in the people he admired has been well documented. His "code heroes" exemplify American values of honor, courage, and endurance in a chaotic world of loss and destruction, where pre–World War I values have been displaced by "a world in which what has made a man a potent being, a conqueror of nature, no longer matters" (Wilentz 192). Thus, Hemingway always returns to the America he loved.

However, this identification with the American culture is complicated by Hemingway's clear avowals of appreciation for and desire to belong to other cultures. This can be seen in *A Moveable Feast* in which Hemingway talks almost possessively about Paris: "We looked and there it all was: our river and our city and this island of our city" (56). A sense of ownership exists in the way he refers to the city and its various occupants: "[But] for a long time it was enough just to be back in our part of Paris and away from the tracks and to bet on our own life and work, and on the painters that you knew" (63). The use of "our" in referring to Paris underlines the yearning that Hemingway had for an Other place. This connection and empathy with other sociocultural spaces can also be seen in Hemingway's insistence that he belonged to Native American (Ojibwe in Nick Adams stories), Spanish (Jake Barnes in *The Sun Also Rises* and Robert Jordan in *For Whom the Bell Tolls*), and African (Wakamba tribe in *Green Hills of Africa*). For Hemingway, identification with the Other cultures was a means of subverting oppressive and rapidly changing mainstream American culture. Indeed, James Mellow states that Hemingway's claim to be Native American was a form of rebellion against the oppressive societal structures that were surrounding him. By identifying with an Other group, Hemingway seemingly found an escape to a less restrictive and limiting cultural ethos.

Hemingway, therefore, by identifying with multiple cultures/races, situates himself in a polyvocal immigrant space that negates essentialist identity structures. Discussing his frequent movements between different cultures, he writes in *A Moveable Feast*:

> I walked down past the Lycée Henri Quatre and the ancient church of St.-Étienne-du-Mont and the windswept Place du Panthéon. I ordered a café au lait. The waiter brought it and I took out a notebook from the pocket of the coat and a pencil and started to write. I was writing about Michigan and since it was a wild, cold, blowing day it was that sort of day in the story. I had already seen the end of fall come through boyhood, youth and young manhood, and in one place you could write about it better than in another. *That was called transplanting yourself,* I thought, and it could be as necessary with people as with other sorts of growing things. But in the story the boys were drinking and this made me thirsty and I ordered a rum St. James. (5; emphasis added)

The analogy of "transplanting" that Hemingway introduces here is indicative of the complexity of his relationship not only to America but also to the other adopted countries. For in that very process, the transplanted object, while growing and flourishing in Other soil, also depends on the birth soil for definition and coherence. Therefore, the constant efforts Hemingway makes to change and adapt to new cultural/racial structures depend on his ability to identify and empathize with the Other.

The literary and stylistic experiments in Hemingway's work reflect his dilemma of negotiating between the two realities, and that dilemma underlies the basic tension in his creation of the Self in an increasingly multicultural and unstable framework of power. Consequently, the plot, characters, and techniques in Hemingway's works reflect multiple spaces of identification with the Other. As a result, Hemingway's works provide a useful point of departure for discussions on race and culture centered on the Self/Other negotiations.

Students in the classrooms today increasingly inhabit a world that resembles a diaspora. They are constantly being introduced to new information, knowledge, and people. Many react with panic and resort to prejudice and bias toward the Other to reestablish their sense of Self. The polyvocal immigrant tradition present in texts like *A Moveable Feast* and *A Farewell to Arms* create a space where students can identify with the experience of the new, the Other. This identification is central in helping students to see connections between their own life experiences and those they encounter in Hemingway's work to create secure, empathic identities.

Context and Text

The exercises in this section are geared toward a fifty-minute class in any level of undergraduate or graduate study. The degree of difficulty in the diction of the exercise prompts and discussion would vary according to the level at which the class is being taught and is at the teacher's discretion. These exercises include both a written component and class discussion and have an explicit focus on race/culture. The students are encouraged to express their views on the discussed subject. The exercises presented here are a preview to the vast possibility of assignments that can be created to cultivate secure, empathic identities in students.

The core works used for these exercises are Hemingway's *A Moveable Feast* and *A Farewell to Arms*. Posthumously published in 1964, *A Moveable Feast* is Hemingway's memoir of his Paris days while *A Farewell to Arms* (1929) comes out of his experiences as an ambulance driver during the Italian campaign of World War I. Both of these works deal with issues of culture/race and the negotiations that the characters must engage in to survive in their world. This makes the two works a stimulating point of departure for discussions on the Self and Other.

Exercise 1

Part A: Vividly describe an incident in Hemingway's *A Farewell to Arms* that reminds you of a past experience with a racial Other and that aroused strong emotions in you. This incident does not have to be a real-life interaction with the Other. It could be a reaction to something you saw or read. It could be something like the racial confusion that arose out of the Milanese Barber's misunderstanding of Frederick Henry's nationality. How did you feel when a similar incident occurred to you? Did you feel threatened, angry, or saddened? How did you act—defensively, indifferently? What was your body posture—that is, were your fists clenched or did you turn away from the Other? What were your facial features? Did you speak? Did the words convey your emotions?

Part B: How do you feel now reading about this incident in the novel? Does it evoke similar emotions as when you went through the experience? What are the details that make the scene in the novel similar to your experience—the emotions, the mental state, the words, and so on? What do you feel for the character going through the similar experience? Do you feel compassion or indifference? Explain why you feel what you feel.

Class Discussion: Why do you think that you feel indifference or compassion for a character very different from you and with whom you probably have no similarity other than going through a comparable situation? Would you help that character feel better if he or she were here now? What steps would you take to help the person?

Explanation: The first set of questions are structured so that they engage all the affective, physiological, imagistic, and linguistic registers in the students and evoke some basic memories from their past. The students' memories must be from an incident that they react emotionally to every time they read the incident in the novel. This would allow the students to be more fully engaged in the process while focusing on minute details that will allow them to find similarities with the Other. It would further counteract any possible danger of the reading being tinged with past prejudices. With the students' attention on the minutest details of the verbal and nonverbal cues that Hemingway provides, it would provide them with information that would reduce the possibility of filling the gaps with their own collected and probably biased knowledge.

The second part of the exercise is geared toward identifying the character in the incident for whom they feel the most concern. This is possible when they separate their emotions of the past from the present and become aware of the similarities of their present distress to the character's feelings. The analysis of their own emotions will lead students to see the conscious or unconscious connections between the Self and the Other. This is a critical step in expanding empathic distress from a character in the novel to a person in real life as it involves an analysis and reflection of their own cognitive process, which leads to prosocial action.

The discussion, therefore, attempts to motivate the students to realize the similarity of the human experience (between Hemingway's life or his characters and their own). Their involuntary identification with a character with whom they would not have identified with otherwise is indicative of how people from all groups feel the same basic emotions in response to similar experiences like birth, death, hunger, etc. People, whether they belong to the in-group or out-group, are the same. The expanding circle of empathy, however, must result in action. The discussion further attempts to motivate the students to transform their empathic distress into action that would help cultural/racial Others.

The teacher can play an instrumental role in pointing out the structural similarity of the basic human emotions and experiences and providing information to fill the gap. This exercise provides opportunities for addressing biases based on familiarity and presence of the Other here and now. These biases appear in the retrieval process of their own memories, which a student has to conjure in making connections between the Self and the Other and expanding their circle of empathy. The effectiveness of this exercise increases if it is accompanied by a visual text (such as the 1957 movie of *A Farewell to Arms*) in which the students can see the character's facial cues and body postures.

Exercise 2

Describe an incident from Hemingway's *A Moveable Feast* that deals with interactions between characters of differing races/cultures. This incident must be something that you can vividly picture in your head and distresses you. What in the incident arouses distress? Whom do you feel bad for? What verbal and nonverbal cues do you get that allow you to imagine and feel the character's distress? What words and images are being used that make you feel distressed? How is the victim feeling—secure or insecure? Why do you feel distress when you read this scene? Is there a specific word that arouses distress? Does it remind you of something in your own life? What are the words and images that you identify with and connect to your own past experience?

Class discussion: How does the use of specific words arouse certain emotions in you—that is, *birth* arousing joy, *separation* arousing sorrow, and so on? Do these words always arouse the same emotions in you? Since the character whom you feel bad for in the scene is a distant Other, would you be willing to help this character?

Explanation: This exercise attempts to diminish bias arising out of difference in physical bodies and features of the cultural/racial Other by centering the student's attention on linguistic codes, which are universal. Hemingway presents many subtle anecdotes that separate the physicality and social customs between cultures/races that he identifies with and those that he sees as the Other. The students through this exercise will not only be able to identify with an expanding circle of people but also effectively articulate and interpret Others' cues to maintain a secure sense of Self.

The written part of the exercise asks the students to focus on a distressing event in the book that they can visualize. The ability to imagine the situation of the Other and simulate their identity state through verbal cues is crucial in arousing empathy and reducing bias. Developing imagination in the students by asking them to focus on the minute verbal and nonverbal traits of the character encourages them to connect the information that they are getting from *A Moveable Feast* to their past experiences. The identification and recognition of similarity between the Self and Other's emotional state can lead to the student's awareness that most people react to similar situations in an analogous way. This creates greater empathic distress and a desire to alleviate the Other's pain with the expansion of the in-group of the Self.

The class discussion encourages the students to investigate the connection of words with the arousal of certain emotions. For instance, the word *separation* usually stirs the emotions of unhappiness, sorrow, or dread. Indeed, this exercise is especially useful in Hemingway because of the careful crafting of his stylistic and linguistic experiments. By allowing students to analyze the word/emotion pairings, the discussion focuses on how particular properties of words have become conditioned stimuli. This is especially important in any discussions of prejudice as people tend to react automatically with bias in response to certain words (like *black, white, affirmative action,* and so on) without analyzing all the information. By rethinking the connection between words and emotions, students will be more open to the possibility of accepting new readings that are separate from their own. It would allow them to analyze and reevaluate not only their own pairings but also Hemingway's. Thus, the acceptance of multiple interpretations would give students a bigger repertoire for future retrieval and make them more capable of reading the emotion/word pairings that are unconditioned for them. Teachers, therefore, can model their exercises to encourage students to enhance their skills in decoding verbal messages from the Other and in communicating their own emotional states as well. This is a crucial step in not only expanding the circle of empathy but also creating and sustaining a secure identity in the students to lead to prosocial action.

Conclusion

Hemingway creates a polyvocal immigrant space in his life as well as in his works, subverting essentialist cultural/racial enunciations. Teachers can utilize the unique unhyphenated perspective evident in *A Moveable Feast* and *A Farewell to Arms* not only to create strategies within the classroom that sustain the student's secure identity but also to lead to increasing empathy for the Other. The pedagogical strategies presented here facilitate the development of complex identity contents in the students to make them more open to identifying commonalities between the Self and Other based on universal affective states and life conditions and to taking practical steps to alleviate the Other's suffering. By encouraging the students to develop complex identity components that enable them to see similarities with the Other, as evident in Hemingway, the pedagogy thus promotes greater understanding among people and the desire to engage in prosocial thinking and action.

Notes

1. For further discussion on Hemingway's complex negotiation of his racial identity as representative of a national apprehension, see Dudley.

2. For more on the research on the development of empathic modes in children, consult Meltzoff; Reissland; Haviland and Lelwica; and Termine and Izard.

3. Eby points out that "Hemingway's reign as a hairy-chested icon of American masculinity is coming to an end" (3) with the rethinking of gender roles in his works.

Blooming Hemingway

Cam Cobb and Michael K. Potter

While Hemingway stories could be used to examine creative writing as well as stylistic shifts in literature, they could also be used to delve into matters of sociology. In this essay, we discuss how "The Doctor and the Doctor's Wife" (hereafter *TDDW*) could be used to foster learning experiences that are rooted in critical pedagogy.[1] First published in the *Transatlantic Review* in 1924, *TDDW* is presently available in numerous Hemingway collections. Because the story raises questions about racial identity and power in society, it is useful as both an object of study and a teaching tool. The core question we aim to address is: *How might educators develop rich learning outcomes and meaningful experiences rooted in critical pedagogy when exploring TDDW?* To address this question, we have divided the essay into six segments, including Active Learning, Learning Outcomes, "The Doctor and the Doctor's Wife," Developing Learning Outcomes for *TDDW*, From Learning Outcomes to Experiences, and Multiple Lens Portfolio.

1. Active Learning

Because there are different—and sometimes conflicting—views of learning, the way in which teaching is defined and practiced often varies. At times, this variance can be profound. According to John Biggs, "[T]wo broad theoretical traditions can be distinguished" in education, namely objectivism and constructivism. In the first tradition, which is objectivist in nature, "knowledge exists independently of the knower, and understanding is coming to know that which already exists." From this perspective, "knowledge is seen as decontextualized," and "teaching is a matter of transmitting this knowledge, learning of receiving it accurately, storing it, and using it appropriately" ("Enhancing Teaching" 347). Concerned with this approach, Paulo Freire described it as a system where students "patiently receive, memorize, and repeat" the "communiqués" of teachers. He called it the banking concept of education (72). If an educator were to apply an objectivist approach to teaching Hemingway, she would act as a conduit, relaying details about such topics as writing style and social context to a group of learners.

Rejecting the objectivist tradition, constructivists view education as an interaction among teachers, learners, and a specific subject area.[2] These learning interactions are seen as being "central in the creation of meaning" where both educators and students draw from newly acquired knowledge, as well as newly developed skills, to solve problems and rethink their perspectives of the world (Biggs, "Enhancing Teaching" 248). To foster meaningful learning interactions, John Dewey reasoned that teachers should draw from the experiences of learners. He argued that teachers need to "select those things within the range of existing experience that have the promise and potentiality of presenting new problems which by stimulating new ways of observation and judgment will expand the area of further experience" (*Experience and Education* 75). Stressing the need for reciprocity, Freire presented problem-posing education as an alternative to the banking concept of education. More recently, Richard Mayer argued that, "meaningful learning occurs when students build the knowledge and cognitive processes needed for successful problem solving." Problem solving, in Mayer's view, "involves devising a way of achieving a goal that one has never previously achieved" (227).

We have opened with a brief overview of active learning because it reminds us that learner engagement is central to our work. And the teaching approach we outline in this essay draws from constructivism, which views teaching and learning as an interaction. With constructivism in mind, an important question to ponder is: *How are we to foster active learning experiences that engage students when using TDDW to explore questions of racial identity and power in society?*

2. Learning Outcomes

Learning outcomes articulate what it is students are expected to gain from a given learning experience. A learning experience might be an activity, such as a student-led discussion, an inquiry-based project, or a peer-feedback conferencing session linked to a piece of writing. On a larger scale, a learning experience might be viewed as a lesson, a course, or even an entire program. Whatever the learning experience might be, there will be, at its core, a set of outcomes that students are expected to attain through their participation in the experience. These learning outcomes provide a foundation for developing activities and assessments that support the experience.

Learning outcomes are important because they represent a way for educators to *start* thinking about the teaching-learning process. As educators begin to formulate learning outcomes, they ask questions about purpose, context, and suitability. Some of these questions include: *What is the purpose of this class? Who are the students? Why are they here? What do they hope to gain from this experience? What sorts of skills do these students need to develop within the context of our class?* Carefully reflecting on these questions helps educators to determine what sorts of learning experiences would make sense for a given lesson or series of lessons. As we relate the matter of learning outcomes to *TDDW*, we might ask ourselves: *If one were to use TDDW to foster learning experiences that delve into sociological issues, what sorts of learning outcomes would make sense for these students?*

3. "The Doctor and the Doctor's Wife"

TDDW opens with three men stepping onto Dr. Adams's property. The men are Dick Boulton, his son Eddy, and Billy Tabeshaw. According to the narrator, the three "came from the Indian camp to cut up logs for Nick's father" (*Nick Adams Stories* 22). When describing the men, the narrator adds that, "Dick was a half-breed and many of the farmers around the lake believed he was really a white man" (23). Billy is Ojibwe.[3] The three men bring with them a variety of tools and have come to carry out a chore for the doctor. Because the doctor tended to Dick's wife while she had pneumonia, Dick agreed to make cordwood out of four large beech logs that are by the lake near the doctor's cottage. Early in the story, the narrator explains, "[T]he logs had been lost from the big log booms that were towed down the lake to the mill" (22). Before Dick begins his work, he says to the doctor, "Well Doc [. . .] that's a nice lot of timber you've stolen." When the doctor replies that it's driftwood, Dick asks his helpers to wash the logs in the lake. After washing off the sawdust and sand, they soon discover markings that indicate the wood belongs to a company called White and McNally. The doctor tells Dick, "You'd better not saw it up then." Dick replies, "Don't get huffy. I don't care who you steal from" (23–24).

In a fit of anger, the doctor responds, "If you think the logs are stolen, leave them alone and take your tools back to the camp." His face was red. "Don't go off at half cock, Doc," Dick calmly replies. "You know they're stolen as well as I do. It don't make any difference to me." When Dick continues to address the doctor as "Doc," Dr. Adams threatens, "If you call me Doc once again, I'll knock your eye teeth down your throat." The narrator describes Dick as a "big man" who "knew how big a man he was" and "liked to get into fights." In responding to the doctor's threat, Dick counters, "Oh, no, you won't, Doc." After a tense moment, Dr. Adams turns around, walks up the hill, and steps into his cottage. Dick says something in Ojibwe, which prompts his son to laugh out loud. Billy Tabeshaw did not laugh, and although he did not understand English, "he had sweat all the time the row was going on." The three men then "walked up past the cottage and out the back gate into the woods" (24). Dick leaves the gate open and Billy goes back and fastens it shut.

The doctor's wife, who is lying in bed, asks what the matter is, and the doctor tells her he had an argument with Dick. When he speculates that Dick caused the row to get out of work, his wife replies, "I really don't think that anyone would really do a thing like that" (26). As Dick converses with his wife, who remains in bed, he meticulously cleans a shotgun and then leans it behind a dresser. When he leaves to go for a walk, his wife asks him to send their son, Nick, to see her. The doctor apologizes to his wife after slamming the door on his way out and, after encountering his son, the two go for a walk.

Critiques of *TDDW* have reflected shifts in literary criticism over time. While early analyses tended to focus on the perspective of Nick Adams and the Hemingway *code hero*,[4] more recent studies have delved further into the sociological dimensions of the story. Key themes critics have explored in recent years include ownership, language, and racial identity.

Ownership—What do the beech logs tell us about conquest? What do they say about capitalism? And who *really* owns them? As Thomas Strychacz observed, "The mark of the scaler's hammer in the log shows that it belongs to "White" and "McNally" (59). Aware that he doesn't own the logs, "Dr. Adams chooses to rename the wood, altering its status from 'timber,' which entails value and ownership, to 'driftwood,' implying a freedom from the rules of legal possession" (Strong 23). The doctor's lack of ownership ultimately "gives rise to a double irony [. . .] in the sense that White has stolen from the Indian, but the immorality of the act comes home to the doctor only in the idea of a white stealing from White." Early in the story, "with the fact of appropriation suddenly evident, the moral superiority of white culture is shown to be a mere covering for an aggressive exploitation of natural resources" (Strychacz 59).

Language—When Dick Boulton verbally challenges the doctor, calling attention to his dishonesty, Dr. Adams tells him not to "talk that way" (*NAS* 23). In a sense, the doctor is attempting to control Dick's use of language (Dudley 45). But Dr. Adams's attempts at manipulation are unsuccessful. As Amy Strong noted, "Not only does Dick Boulton make the doctor back down, but he uses Ojibway, a language unfamiliar to Dr. Adams, to mock him." Consequently, the confrontation between Dick and Dr. Adams "presents an utter reversal of power relations, where the dominant language, or, the language of dominance, has lost its force" (Strong 22). As the conflict unfolds, Dr. Adams "is exposed, by Dick Boulton, for what he is (or at least what Boulton would have him be): a thief, a liar, and a flawed man" (Dudley 37). Summing up the exchange, Marc Kevin Dudley noted that Boulton "outwits and out-talks the doctor, using words as weapons" (49).

Racial Identity—*TDDW* presents race as a fluid social construct. Dick Boulton, a man who lives among Ojibwe, code switches between English and Ojibwe with ease and is perceived by the farmers around the lake as a "white man" (*NAS* 23). But he isn't the only character to transgress race in the story. "During the confrontation," Amy Strong noted, "the doctor's face presumably because of his embarrassment and anger, has turned red." The heated exchange thus "dislodges the most stubborn racial marker of all—skin color." The argument between Dr. Adams (a dishonest employer) and Dick Boulton (a laborer who publically confronts his employer), "forces social relations into the realm of violence, at once exposing and challenging the artificiality of power relations based on essentialist notions of racial difference" (25). In explicitly calling attention to the doctor's act of theft, "Boulton's agency expands beyond the limited prescriptive radius of the other. Unspoken rules of decorum become figurative lines in the sand dividing white from red." By leaving the doctor's gate open at the end of the story, Boulton further flouts protocol. Ultimately, "with power markers blurred, Hemingway shows us that dividing lines of race conflate, and the two men [. . .] become harder to differentiate" (Dudley 43, 38, 43).

4. Developing Learning Outcomes for *TDDW*

In this segment, we first develop a draft set of learning outcomes, which could help to guide educators when using the *TDDW*. We then use Bloom's Revised Taxonomy to develop a second draft of the learning outcomes and to better ensure that they delve into higher order thinking skills. Drawing from critical pedagogy, we design a third draft of the learning outcomes to deepen their link to social justice learning.

Three outcomes that could support *TDDW* are (1) *Identify* the main idea of short stories, (2) *Summarize* the key events in short stories, and (3) *Create* works of literary criticism that *evaluate* short stories. It is important to note the verbs we have used in these learning outcomes. In the first outcome, we ask students to *identify*. But what sort of skills should students use when identifying the main idea? And how should students justify their choice? One way to enhance this learning outcome would be to better indicate how students are expected to identify the main idea. The second learning outcome asks students to *summarize* events. While summarizing is an important skill, it does not ask students to use critical thinking skills. One possible way to enhance this learning outcome would be to ask students to summarize for a certain purpose. The third outcome, which asks students to *create/evaluate*, invites students to use higher-order thinking skills. But it lacks detail. Just what sort of a piece of literary criticism are students expected to create, and what exactly constitutes well-reasoned evaluation? Specifying the piece of criticism that students are to create and indicating what they are expected to evaluate in the short story would clarify the third learning outcome.

Enriching the Outcomes—Bloom's Revised Taxonomy

In 1956, an American-based group of curriculum theorists, led by Benjamin Bloom, proposed a vision of the cognitive domain of learning. It came to be known as Bloom's Taxonomy. In 2001, David Krathwohl collaborated with Lorin Anderson to transform the initial taxonomy into Bloom's Revised Taxonomy. This new format includes six levels within the cognitive domain, including remembering, understanding, applying, analyzing, evaluating, and creating. It also adds knowledge as a multileveled second dimension. Four aspects of knowledge within the revised taxonomy include factual, conceptual, procedural, and metacognitive knowledge (Krathwohl 214–15).

With Bloom's Revised Taxonomy in mind, we have modified the outcomes and added a fourth. The second draft of the outcomes reads as follows: (1) *Derive* the main idea of short stories from such aspects as plot, character, and setting; (2) *Relate* the events in short stories to the main idea of the story; (3) *Create* pieces of persuasive writing that *evaluate* clarity of the main idea of the story as well as the writer's technique in conveying the main idea; and (4) *Identify* and *evaluate* strategies used to *conduct* a literary analysis within the body of the analysis.

To consider how the first two outcomes have been changed, we need to pay close attention to the verbs. Rather than asking students to *identify* and *summarize*, students are now asked to *derive* and *relate*. While this might appear to be a small difference, it isn't. Deriving and relating are different actions, and they require more complex thought processes. Simply put, they ask students to deepen their inquiry into the story. And these new verbs add detail about what students are expected to learn and demonstrate. The revised third learning outcome makes use of the same initial two verbs (*create, evaluate*), but adds the verb *conduct* to indicate what it is the students are to *create* and what they are to *evaluate*. While we have added detail to the first three learning outcomes, we have attempted to do so without limiting the creativity of students. We have also added detail to counter the vagueness—and potential confusion—that hindered the first draft of the learning outcomes. In composing a fourth outcome, which invites students to reflect on their own thought processes, we have added a metacognitive element to the experience.

This second draft of learning outcomes invites students to consider a variety of questions, including: *What is the main idea of TDDW? How do the plot, characters, and setting connect to the main idea of the story? How might I persuasively write about the story? What strategies and evidence will I use to write about the story's main idea? How might I discuss my own use of strategies and evidence in my analysis of the story?* Yet while these are worthy questions to explore, they do not touch on sociological dimensions of the story.

Further Enriching the Outcomes—Critical Pedagogy

To further enrich the learning outcomes, we will apply the lens of critical pedagogy. Critical pedagogy is "a school of thought ... steeped in a long tradition of critical social thought and progressive educational movements" (Darder 90). According to Antonia Darder, it "links the practice of schooling to democratic principles of society and to transformative social action" (90). Key principles that underpin critical pedagogy include resistance and counter hegemony (90–94). In the early 1990s, James Banks developed a lens to help educators foster social justice education. Within Banks's framework are five core dimensions of learning, including: content integration, knowledge construction, prejudice reduction, equitable pedagogy, and empowering school culture and social structure (22–28). Transformative critical knowledge action is an important concept that underpins Banks's model because it urges educators and students not only to recognize but also to address the socially constructed nature of knowledge and privilege. It also urges people to challenge racial, economic, and other inequities that surround them. In Banks's view, "multicultural education views citizen action to improve society as an integral part of education in a democracy; it links knowledge, values, empowerment, and action" (23).

With the Banks's model in mind, we have revised the four learning outcomes and added aspects of social justice thinking-action. The third draft of the learning outcomes are as follows: (1) *Derive* the main idea of short stories from such aspects as plot, character, and setting; (2) *Relate* the events in short stories to the main idea of the story; (3) *Create* works of literary criticism that *compare* events in short stories to the wider social context within which the story is set; and (4) *Identify* and *evaluate* strategies used to *conduct sociological analyses* with the body of literary analyses. In developing this third draft of the learning outcomes, we have left the first two outcomes alone and have made important revisions to the second two. The third learning outcome now asks students to examine stories to make comparisons to the larger sociological context. To deepen the call for metacognitive thinking, the fourth learning outcome now asks students to articulate *how* they use stories to draw conclusions about a sociological context.

Because this third draft of learning outcomes asks students to make sociological connections, it is now necessary to explore matters of race and power within the story as well as the context within which the story takes place. And key questions that might arise from this new set of learning outcomes include: *What is racial identity? How is it constructed and portrayed in TDDW? How does racial identity affect one's perceived status in the story? What are the perspectives of the Ojibwe in the story? What sorts of barriers do they face? How might Dr. Adams have come to own land that had once belonged to the Ojibwe? What role did race, gender, and other factors play in determining ownership in early twentieth-century America? What happened in the early 1900s when laborers challenged their employers on moral grounds? How did racial conflicts, at times, lead to violence in the early 1900s? How was male violence perceived?* As these questions indicate, *TDDW* invites a wide range of inquiries into the world in which Dr. Adams and Dick Boulton lived. Making slight adjustments to these questions could lead educators and students to inquire into matters of racial identity and power in our present world.

5. From Learning Outcomes to Experiences

In the previous four segments of this essay, we demonstrated how learning outcomes might be formulated and then refined to intersect social justice with deep learning. Through this process, we developed learning outcomes that could guide educators as they use *TDDW* to foster experiences rooted in critical pedagogy. In the fifth and sixth segments of this essay we illustrate how those outcomes could be put into practice through a sequence of scaffolded opportunities to learn though inquiry and engagement. We have named this project the Multiple Lens Portfolio.

The task before us is to suggest possible learning experiences for the learning outcomes created for a course using *TDDW*. We have the following set of learning outcomes (slightly reworded): (1) *Derive* the main idea of short stories from such aspects as plot, character, and setting; (2) *Relate* the events in short stories to the main idea of the story; (3) *Create* pieces of persuasive writing that *compare* events in short stories to the wider social context within which the story is set; and (4) *Identify* and *evaluate* strategies used to *conduct* sociological analyses within pieces of persuasive writing.

Learning Context

In devising possible learning experiences for these outcomes, we need to understand their purposes, the pedagogical context in which they are to be achieved, and the relevant characteristics of our expected students (such as anticipated prior knowledge and maturity/educational level). Unless we consider the purposes, the achievement of any set of learning outcomes may be counterproductive. If we ignore pedagogical context, we lack guidance as to the range of learning experiences from which me may draw, as some will reinforce our purposes and others will not. Consideration of relevant student characteristics is necessary to ensure that learning experiences are properly scaffolded and expect neither too much nor too little.

The sequence of learning experiences outlined in this essay has been designed for a first-year undergraduate course in English literature. We might expect it to be a large class, with an enrollment of approximately one hundred students, though the sequence we propose could be adapted for larger or smaller classes. With a class of this size, we might also expect that there is at least one graduate assistant (GA) to collaborate on program development, teaching, and assessment. Most students in this class will be in their first year of university. All the students will have studied literature in high school and will have had some in writing pieces of literary analysis. The experiences that students have had in examining literature, and the skills they possess in analyzing literature, will undoubtedly be varied. Additionally, we might reasonably expect that while some of the students enrolled in this course will have been exposed to social justice learning (through experiences rooted in such pedagogies as critical pedagogy and feminist pedagogy), others will have not been. While many of these students will have studied Hemingway in high school, it is important to note that some will not have had any experience in reading or analyzing his work.

Additionally, depending on the university community in which this course it taught, it is quite possible that the class would contain students from diverse cultural and linguistic backgrounds, many of whom might have experience with short stories and literary analysis in a language other than English, using conventions that differ from those in Anglo-American narrative. Consequently, for students in this first-year undergraduate course, learning about Hemingway and social justice might be a new experience, and it is important to keep this in mind as we consider how to pose reasonable challenges that engage *all* learners.

Scaffolding Learning

When planning learning experiences, it is helpful to arrange the set of learning outcomes in order of their complexity. This helps one plan learning experiences that gradually increase in difficulty and prevents situations in which students are expected to learn y before learning its prerequisite, x. A plan for scaffolded learning in the Multiple Lens Portfolio will involve reformulating and supplementing the above learning outcomes as follows: (1) *Derive* main ideas of short stories from plot, character, and setting; (2) *Relate* events in short stories to their main ideas; (3) *Create* pieces of persuasive writing that *evaluate* clarity of main ideas and writers' technique; (4) *Create* pieces of persuasive writing that *compare* events in short stories to the wider social context within which the story is set; and (5) *Identify* and *evaluate* strategies used to *conduct* sociological literary analyses.

The learning outcomes describe, at a minimum level, what students will need to learn to excel in the course: each verb in the learning outcome denotes something that needs to be learned, ideally actively, and involving ample feedback. Learning outcomes that incline us wholly toward passive modes of instruction are rare, as most desired learning involves abilities that extend beyond rote memorization and mere listening. But it is important to interrogate the learning outcomes to uncover what they involve, for the learning outcomes may assume knowledge and abilities that are not made explicit. Let's try this with one of the outcomes.

Working from the most complex learning outcome, for instance, we should ask: *What must students know to identify and evaluate strategies used to conduct sociological literary analyses?* Surely, they must be able to identify strategies used to conduct a literary analysis, which is captured in another part of this learning outcome, placed earlier in the sequence. To do that, they must also know what literary analysis is, what it is intended to accomplish, and at least some of its major terms and techniques. That set of items is likely to include the learning captured in the first two outcomes in the sequence. But there is still a missing component: what it means to evaluate strategies—in particular, what it means to evaluate strategies *well*.

Now that we have analyzed the outcome into its components and assumptions, the question is: *What is likely to help students learn these things?* The standard approach to teaching students terms and techniques is through a combination of lectures and readings—which may have a place in an overall set of learning experiences but are, alone, insufficient. The Multiple Lens Portfolio is a more active approach to helping students achieve the learning outcomes, consistent with constructivism and critical pedagogy, and likelier than standard approaches to be effective.

6. Multiple Lens Portfolio

Through the remainder of this essay we will outline the Multiple Lens Portfolio, a series of learning experiences designed to activate and facilitate the above-listed learning outcomes. The Multiple Lens Portfolio presents an opportunity to foster literary analysis that intermingles with social justice thinking. The activities within the project will unfold over eight lessons, and their sequential nature will gradually add complexity and scaffold skill development.[5] Students will come to each of the lessons having read (or reread) *TDDW*. The story will act as a living artifact that will be examined multiple times, on different levels, and in different ways. It is an artifact because it comes from a certain time and context. It is a living artifact because, as readers, we respond to the story in our own personal ways, as we make connections to other things we have read, observed, or experienced in our own lives.

Note that the Multiple Lens Portfolio is both a sequence of learning experiences and a set of assessment tasks. The boundary between learning experiences and assessment tasks is blurred in the learning paradigm, as assessment is no longer conceived as something that takes place when learning is over, but rather as part of the sequence of learning experiences (Barr and Tagg 27, 12–25). Drawing from contemporary scholarship, we posit that the best approaches to assessment fulfill three functions: (1) They facilitate learning, (2) They reliably and validly judge the sorts of learning we care about most, and (3) They maintain and promote high standards (Joughin, "Introduction" xx). The Multiple Lens Portfolio is intended to fulfill these functions. Assessment drives learning.

Student approaches to learning experiences is shaped, in large part, by how they believe they will be assessed. Furthermore, high-quality assessment tasks are themselves learning experiences.

Each item in the Multiple Lens Portfolio is an assessment task, and the portfolio is a holistic assessment task in which already completed work is organized and presented as a coherent set. But the completion of each of those items is also a learning experience, or set of learning experiences, used as the "lessons" of the course. Class time is devoted to them. The experience of being in the course will feature very little passivity or rote learning, consistent with the constructivist and critical pedagogy principles that informed the development of the learning outcomes.

Note that the Multiple Lens Portfolio continually leads students to reflect. The sort of reflection involved is intended to be what Biggs and Tang call "transformative reflection"—a means to develop and redefine oneself through careful, deliberate, thought (43).[6] This sort of reflection potentially incorporates Dewey's five aspects of reflective thinking: reflexive anticipation of ways to deal with a dissonant experience, intellectualization of the dissonant experience into a problem to be solved, formulation of hypotheses to inform potential solutions, reformulation of hypotheses in light of new information, and empirical or imaginative testing of, or experimentation with, hypotheses (Dewey, *How We Think* 199–209). All these aspects can be incorporated into the reflections in the Multiple Lens Portfolio using the philosophical model of thought experiments.

We will open the project by explaining to students (1) what the project entails, (2) how their work will be assessed, and (3) which portfolio items they will develop (both individually and in their small groups). We will also instruct students not only to dig deep into a Hemingway story (*TDDW*) but also to develop a portfolio that will ultimately indicate how they relate to the story, how they make connections to their own lives, and how they analyze the story on both a literary and sociological level.[7]

This approach helps us not only to achieve the critical pedagogy aims of the course but also to deepen student learning. According to the Structure of Observed Learning Outcomes (SOLO) taxonomy, qualitative gains in learning are a function of the number and complexity of connections students make (Biggs and Collis).[8] By connecting ideas and experiences with each other, students' understanding of those ideas deepens to the point at which they start using those ideas to make sense of their world, thus facilitating transfer of learning beyond the course and, ideally, beyond the program. The ultimate goal is to help students advance to the Extended Abstract level of understanding, at which point they start using the ideas they are learning in new situations and autonomously draw connections between them and other facets of their lives, independent of a teacher's prompting.

Crucial to the development of such higher-level understanding is the encouragement of deep approaches to learning.[9] The Multiple Lens Portfolio aims to accomplish this by consistently pushing students to make connections, find relationships, see the big picture, interpret what they learn through the lenses of their own experiences, analyze and synthesize the ideas they encounter, evaluate approaches, take some risks, learn and use deep-learning approaches and meta-cognitive habits (Bransford, Brown, and Cocking; Donovan and Bransford), take advantage of the self-referral effect, over-learn key ideas (Svinicki), requiring students to integrate domains of learning (cognitive, performative, and affective), and otherwise construct meaning from *TDDW*. This should help students learn at a level that results in long-term retention, transfer, and greater facility in using what they have learned when the course is over.[10] These deep learning goals are supported by the integration of learning experiences and assessment, which should avoid the common situation in which positive changes to learning experiences are undone by reliance on superficial and traditional assessment tasks.

Rooted in deep learning, the Multiple Lens Portfolio is intended to exemplify the "Seven Principles for Good Practice in Undergraduate Education" (Chickering and Gamson). It encourages frequent contact between students, their teacher, and their GA by using class time for active project-oriented learning (what has been called the "flipped classroom"). The group approach encourages reciprocity and cooperation among students. It is dominated by active-learning approaches rather than passive sitting and listening. There is ample opportunity for prompt and frequent feedback. Time on task is especially emphasized, as nearly everything that students do is directly relevant to achieving the intended learning outcomes, which communicate high expectations. Finally, the project respects diverse talents and ways of engaging in learning.

At each stage of the project, the degree to which students learn and sustain their motivation will be affected by the kind of feedback they receive from their peers, their GA, and, most importantly, their teacher. It is not enough for students to be given tasks to complete; they need to know what they're doing well, what they need to improve upon, and how they can improve. And this information must be conveyed to them in ways that recognize their status as human beings with emotions, rather than automatons waiting for new commands.

First Lens—Vocabulary Reflection

First Reading (whole class)—Before reading the story to the class, ask students to jot down questions they have about the vocabulary in the story. Inform students that their questions are a part of the "first lens" they are applying to the story. Read the story to the class and then ask students to write down at least one vocabulary-oriented question about the story. Discuss these questions. To encourage students, have numerous questions on hand to promote reflection and dialogue, such as: *What is the vocabulary in this story? How is the vocabulary in the story different from the vocabulary of your world? Why do you think this is so? Which words from the story would you say are no longer used or considered to be socially acceptable? What causes words to become socially acceptable or unacceptable? Why did Hemingway use words such as "half breed" and "Indian" in the story? What was his writing context and what is the context of the story's setting?*

Vocabulary Reflection Activity (individual task)—Instruct students to write a vocabulary reflection of one page. Indicate that the purpose of the reflection is to help them connect *TDDW* to their own personal experiences. Use the following questions as prompts: *When have you encountered a word that made you uncomfortable, in a film, book, or conversation? Explain the circumstances in which you encountered the word. What was the word and why did it make you uncomfortable?* Students begin writing their vocabulary reflections in class. Some may even complete theirs, but all students should be given the opportunity to revise their reflections at home, as reflection benefits from temporal distance. The teacher and GA will monitor the class as they work to converse, pose questions, and provide clarifications and encouragement. Each group should keep the vocabulary reflections of their group members in their group folder. These vocabulary reflections will become portfolio item 1. Tell students that they will add to their group folders as the project unfolds so they should bring their group folder to every lesson. (Online folders are also acceptable for this activity.)

Second Lens—Story Maps

Story Elements Lesson (whole class)—Ask students: *What are the key elements of stories?* Brainstorm a list together, writing students' ideas on a chalkboard, whiteboard, or PowerPoint slide. Follow this warm-up discussion with a brief lesson on story elements. Since part of the goal is to ensure students know the major story elements as recognized in scholarship (such as plot, setting, characters, context), make sure that those are highlighted and drawn from students' suggestions as relevant.

Second Reading (whole class)—Tell students that they will read *TDDW* for a second time in class. Ask them to take notes about the elements of the story as they listen and to reflect on Hemingway's writing technique. Inform students that these notes are a part of the "second lens" they are applying to the story. To help prepare students for this note-taking process, it is important to indicate that they will need to think about the construction of the story and consider how Hemingway designed *TDDW* to communicate elements of the story. Ensure that the brainstormed list of story elements is clearly visible as they take notes, and encourage students to refer back to it. Read the story to the class. To provide further direction, post a sample story map for another Hemingway story. Display and explain the exemplar before they tackle portfolio item 2.

Story Map Preparation Activity (group task)—Students work in their preset groups of four. Each group receives a stack of cue cards (or a pad of sticky notes). On the cue cards, students record information about story elements, such as plot points, setting details, character actions, character perspectives, key dialogue, etc. After students have had enough time to complete this task, they set their cards aside for a moment. Ask the class: *What exactly is a main idea and what does it do?* They may have only vague speculations at this point, but the purpose is to get them thinking about what a main idea might be. After several students have attempted to answer the question, explain to the class that stories, in a sense, could be seen as spider webs where their core elements (refer back to the list of elements the students compiled earlier) interact with one another and all work together to serve the story's main idea. By examining those story elements to see how they work together, we might determine a story's main idea.

Story Map Activity (group task)—Instruct each group to reflect on *TDDW* and determine, in one or two sentences, what they believe the main idea of the story is. To spur the class into thinking about possibilities beyond those considered by their groups, ask groups to share their tentative answers and list them on the board. Distribute a flip chart, markers, and tape to each group, and then provide the following instructions: (1) At the center of the flip chart each group will record its agreed upon main idea (of *TDDW*); (2) Groups then put their cue cards on the flip chart; (3) Using arrows (and perhaps other symbols), groups will illustrate how the elements are connected—and each arrow or symbol may include a word or phrase that explains the connection; (4) Once groups have decided how the elements are related, they will tape their cue cards to the flip chart; (5) Tell the class that these flip charts will become story maps for *TDDW* (and this will become portfolio item 2).

Third Lens—Story Map Reflections

Story Map Reflections (group task)—Each group will collaboratively compose a one-page paper that introduces the story and indicates what their (flip chart) story map depicts. They will (1) Describe what their story map looks like; (2) Outline how they came to design their story map in that way; and (3) Indicate how this story map could help people to understand the main idea of the story, as well as how Hemingway punctuates the main idea through his use of setting, context, character, and plot. Their story map reflections should also clearly indicate how the elements of the story relate to (and interact with) one another, as depicted on their story maps. To provide direction to students, post a sample story map for another Hemingway story—the same story about which you provided the exemplar—to prepare them for portfolio item 2. Display and explain the exemplar before they tackle portfolio item 3. As groups work on their story map reflections, the teacher and GA will circulate the class to ask questions, answer questions, and converse with groups about their work as well as their challenges and strategies. It is also important to offer encouragement while monitoring the class. Groups may finish the first draft of their story map reflections after class, and their story map reflection (a first draft) will become portfolio item 3.

Fourth Lens—Revised Story Map Reflections

Reflective Review Discussion (whole class)—Conduct a reflective review of the previous activities. The following questions can help to guide this reflective process: *What did we do? What did we consider? What questions did we ask? Why did we do those tasks, and what could we learn from them?* Be sure that by the end of the reflective review, students have received a summary of, and rationale for, the activities—either emerging from their responses naturally with prompting from you, or from you if they are reluctant to contribute. Tell students that the next logical step is a revision of their one-page written reflections.

Writer's Checklist (plenary discussion)—Explain that the first step in the revision process will be to devise a writer's checklist. Ask students: *What would a writer's checklist look like?* Through discussion, collaboratively develop and refine a list of questions to help guide their writing. Use the board to ensure everyone in the class can see the questions as they are being collaboratively composed and reworked. Some questions that might be developed for this list include: *What is my core argument? How do I articulate this argument? What sort of evidence do I use to support my core argument? How effective is this evidence?*

How have I organized the main ideas of my reflection? How do I know that this organizational framework makes sense? It is important to remind students that writer's checklist questions should help them to better demonstrate the learning outcomes, so during the revision process refer to the learning outcomes to ensure they are aligned with the questions being developed. Expand on this point by speaking to some key considerations in formulating a work of literary analysis, a piece of persuasive writing, and a clear and well-supported argument. Make sure that the final checklist is on the board and post the checklist to the course website after class. If there isn't a course website, provide a handout.

Revised Story Map Reflections (group task)—Each group will revise its one-page reflection papers using the writer's checklist. Provide time for the groups to begin this process in class, with the expectation that they will finish outside of class. As groups revise their work, the teacher and GA will circulate the room to monitor their progress and converse with them. The revised one-page papers (second draft) will become portfolio item 4.

Fifth Lens—Social Context Artifact I (Social Context Inventory)

During the fifth and sixth activities, artifacts will be used to connect *TDDW* to the larger social milieu within which it is set—and within which it was written. Bear in mind, the story was written by Hemingway in the early 1920s and is set in early 1900s Michigan. An important aspect of the story's sociological dimension involves the identity and position of the Ojibwe in early twentieth-century America. In the fifth activity, the educator will bring in an artifact for the entire class to examine. The artifact could be an image projected on a screen, a short newspaper article from the early 1900s, a photograph (i.e., of an Ojibwe camp), a table (i.e., one that depicts statistics, such as mortality rates), a news article, a land claim description from the early 1900s, a picture of a residential school, a government law, etc. The artifact should tell a story about the social milieu within which the Ojibwe lived in the early 1900s America. Display the image of the artifact on the screen, making sure all students can clearly see it. To encourage students to consider larger sociological dimensions associated with the image, ask a series of questions, including: *What do you see in the image? Who created the image? For what purpose was it created? What information does the image provide about early 1900s America? What information does it provide about Ojibwe life and position in the early 1900s? How can you tell these things?*

Social Context Inventory (group task)—Students are to develop an inventory of social dimensions experienced by the Ojibwe in the early twentieth-century

United States. The inventories might include such information as class differentials; socio-economic status (related to, but distinguishable from class); gender; culture; language; displacement; alienation; marginalization; education; traditions and customs (related to culture, but again distinguishable); religion; orientations; and attitudes. Each group's inventory will become portfolio item 5. For homework, each group is to gather an artifact and bring it to the following lesson. The artifacts that groups gather should provide information about the social milieu of Ojibwe (or other groups of original peoples in North America) in the early 1900s. These artifacts should be images and should be one or two pages. Artifacts might be short newspaper articles (from the era), census data (i.e., tables), court case rulings (no longer than two pages), legislation, or photographs that tell us about the Ojibwe of the early 1900s. Group members must be prepared to describe their artifact and explain what it suggests about social conditions (i.e., racial identity and position) in early twentieth-century America. It is important to note that activity 5 acts as a sort of exemplar that will guide students to complete activity 6.

Sixth Lens—Social Context Artifacts II (Artifact Research Notes)

Setting Up the Room (group task)—Students will be directed to post their artifacts around the classroom or lecture hall at the beginning of the lesson. One representative from each group will go to a wall and post their group's artifact. Each posted artifact must clearly indicate the group's number (i.e., from 1 to 25). At least one group member must stay with their group's artifact during the gallery walk (subsequent activity). The students who stay with their group's artifact must be prepared to explain the artifact.

Gallery Walk (group task)—Once artifacts are posted and each group has at least one member ready to share, the mingling research work will begin. During the gallery walk, group members are to step around the learning space, examine the artifacts, and inquire about them. Before beginning this activity, explain to students that they will gather information about the artifacts. As they mingle and research, they need to take notes that they will then use to develop a piece of writing that connects *TDDW* to its social milieu. The gallery walk is not a competitive activity. Groups work together to make sure they carefully investigate at least three artifacts. Explain to students that they should divvy up the artifacts so each student in the group will gather detailed information about different artifacts.

Artifact Research Notes (group task)—After each group gathers information about three or more artifacts, they should get together and compile their notes in preparation for portfolio item 7. Set a timeline to prepare the class for this transition, and provide time warnings throughout the gallery walk to ensure students are prepared for the transition. Stress that the quality of detail is more important than quantity of artifacts. Students may refine their notes after class if they so desire. Groups are to bring their artifact notes to class for the following activity.

Seventh Lens—*TDDW* Social Context Report

Social Context Report (group task)—In this seventh activity, groups will use their artifact notes from portfolio item 6 to develop a one-page report that explains how *TDDW* links to its social context (more specifically, in relation to the Ojibwe position in early 1900s America). We will call this one-page report the *social context report*. To help guide groups as they develop their social context reports, the teacher and GA will pose numerous questions to the class, such as: *What is freedom? What does it mean to have freedom of religion? What does it mean to have freedom to participate in democratic processes? What was the social status of the Ojibwe in America in the early 1900s? What was their economic status? What was their official status? What sorts of social forces influenced the status of the Ojibwe during this time?*

In order to provide further direction for students, the teacher will present two or three sample paragraphs that use the artifact in different ways. More specifically, the exemplar will use the artifact in portfolio item 5 to draw conclusions about the setting of the story and link the social dynamics in the story to the wider social dynamics in America in the early 1900s. It is important to stress that these sample paragraphs are designed not to provide a template for people to copy but rather to illustrate how the task *might* be approached. Groups will develop a rough draft of their report during the lesson. As groups work collaboratively, the teacher and GA will monitor and converse with students to provide feedback, clarifications, and encouragement. The social context reports, which link three or more artifacts to *TDDW*, may be refined after class. They will become portfolio item 7.

Eighth Lens—Culminating Reflection Activity

Portfolio Learning Reflection (individual-group task)—To begin the eighth activity, groups will review their portfolio items: story map, story map reflections, social context inventory, artifact research notes, and social context report. They will reflect on their process of collaborating and delving into the story's meaning, design, and social milieu. As groups converse, they will reflect on the sociological dimensions of the story. Each group will write a report on its experience. In this report, each group member will provide a personal reflection of approximately one paragraph.

The portfolio learning reflection will become the eighth portfolio item. Key questions to consider during this reflection process include: *What did you learn from the experience of developing each portfolio item? What sorts of strategies did you use to identify (and write about) the main idea of the story? How did you write about the elements of the story as you considered their link to the story's main idea? How did you make connections between the different elements of the story? How did you write about the sociological dimensions of the story? How did you use and "read" different artifacts to better understand and comment on how the Ojibwe are portrayed in the story in relation to their position in the social context within which the story is set?*

Students will be told that they do not need to respond to these questions. Rather, the questions should be used to help groups reflect on their different learning experiences in the Multiple Lens Portfolio project—what they have learned about the story and how that learning happened. Students will begin to develop this paper (portfolio item 8) during the lesson. The teacher and GA will monitor groups as they develop this culminating portfolio item. After the activity, each group will have time to refine its final reflection piece. The entire portfolios will be submitted a week or two after the eighth activity.

Conclusion

In this essay, we have illustrated how a set of learning outcomes might be applied to offer students a chance to learn about *TDDW* in a context rooted in critical pedagogy and structured using constructivist principles. In completing the Multiple Lens Portfolio, students will demonstrate various aspects of social justice thinking. They will also demonstrate an ability to explain their own reasoning processes in critically reading the story and draw conclusions about the story and its social context. The Multiple Lens Portfolio could be utilized as a stand-alone project in the first half of a course. The learner-centered experience would help students develop the foundational skills needed to delve into other stories that invite social justice thinking. If the Multiple Lens Portfolio were used in the first half of a course, then the second half could look at other short stories by Hemingway that explore similar social themes, such as "Indian Camp," "Ten Indians," and "The Indians Moved Away." Rather than aiming to set out a step-by-step series of lessons, our aim has been to illustrate the thought process behind, and core aspects of, how learner-centered experiences could be designed to foster deep learning experiences of critical pedagogy. It is our hope that teachers will draw from this essay as they see fit, using Hemingway stories as both objects and tools of critical pedagogy.

Notes

1. For an overview of critical pedagogy, see Burbules and Berk.

2. For an overview of constructivism, see Biggs, "Enhancing Teaching through Constructive Alignment."

3. While we use the spelling *Ojibwe,* some of the quotations within this essay use the older spelling, *Ojibway.*

4. For an example of this, see DeFalco (33–40).

5. While each activity within the portfolio project could be facilitated in a separate lesson, it is also possible that some of the activities could be combined within lessons. We leave it up to readers to adjust the Multiple Lens Portfolio as they see fit.

6. For a six-point argument for engaging in such reflection that is consistent with critical pedagogy, see Brookfield. For an argument based on the benefits of metalearning, see Biggs, "The Role of Metalearning in Study Processes."

7. Early in this course, the instructor will form twenty-five groups of four. The instructor will review group skills and strategies with the class to help groups proactively address complications that might arise during group work. Some of these skills and strategies include collaboratively identifying tasks and setting timelines and communication expectations.

8. Also see Hattie and Brown.

9. See Marton and Saljo; Ramsden; Biggs, *Student Approaches to Learning and Studying*; Biggs, "What Do Inventories of Students' Learning Processes Really Measure?"; Entwistle; Marton, Hounsell, and Entwistle; Joughin, "Assessment, Learning and Judgement in Higher Education."

10. See Ramsden; Marton, Hounsell, and Entwistle; and Prosser and Trigwell.

Mexicans in Montana
Teaching Hemingway and *Los Betaleberos* in "The Gambler, the Nun, and the Radio"

Sarah Driscoll

Hemingway and Mexicans in Montana

On 22 November 1930, Ernest Hemingway wrote a letter to Archibald MacLeish from St. Vincent Hospital in Billings, Montana. Hemingway had broken his arm during a traffic accident en route from Yellowstone to Billings, where he would remain convalescing for two months. Three years later, Hemingway wrote one of his masterpieces, "The Gambler, the Nun, and the Radio," for *Scribner's Magazine*, a story that he conceived during his hospital stay, as he describes in his long letter to MacLeish. As Hemingway implores when beginning the letter, "[S]it down and write me again, because nothing happens here except the mail comes, and today it stopped coming" (*Selected* 329). As Hemingway proceeds, describing his broken arm which is "coming on fine" after being set at least three times and operated on once (jesting in the meantime about finally being equipped to "land awfully hard on the jaw of Morley Callaghan some day"), it is clear that his convalescence has provided him with the meat and matter for a story to come. Indeed, Hemingway describes a radio in his room, which he employs to listen to American singer Rudy Vallée; a Russian who is across the hall and has been shot in the thigh; and finally, a Mexican, who has been shot in the stomach and "has three tubes in him, and drains a good quality of high-grade pus." Notably, he also chronicles two Mexicans who visit the Mexican patient, one of whom he attests is a "lousy crook," noting that they also visited Hemingway for a good drink of Scotch and rye (331). Similar to what occurs in the short story, the Mexicans promised Hemingway they would return the next day with beer and never did.

At the very least, what Ernest Hemingway's letter to MacLeish reveals is that Hemingway was deeply interested in exploring not only the relationship between the rural West and south of the border in his work but, in particular, the way in which Latin Americans, namely Mexicans, live in the American West. This is important because it underscores Hemingway's broad interest in Latin America, one that transcended his life in Cuba. There has been relatively little scholarship on not only Hemingway's portrayal of Mexican migrant workers but also his trip to Peru in 1956, one that merits attention beyond this particular essay. "The Gambler, the Nun, and the Radio" thus serves as a conduit for initial exploration, one that permits Hemingway scholars a means by which to understand Hemingway's developing interest in Latin America a decade before moving to Cuba in 1940.

The story also documents two central historical components of the 1930s in the United States: the development of what Francisco Balderrama and Raymond Rodríguez describe as "anti-Mexican hysteria," a response to the economic devastation of the Great Depression, and a need to find "a convenient scapegoat" (1). However, despite Americans' attempts to "get rid of the Mexicans" via immigration and deportation measures and new laws designed to restrict job opportunities, Mexican workers persevered, making their way north, even while significant numbers opted to leave the country. And this had been a trend since the beginning of the century, a time during which Mexicans became "the largest new immigrant group in the United States" (Balderrama and Rodríguez 9).

Although the railroad was one of the most promising opportunities for Mexican migrants, the sugar-beet industry provided a new avenue for work. As stated, "Only the sugar beet industry rivaled the railroads in serving as a powerful catalyst in establishing Mexican communities where none had ever existed before." This was particularly the case in the Midwest, where the industry boomed due to the Dingley Tariff Act of 1897, which had levied high taxes on foreign sugar. As evidenced, by 1933, "the Mexican beet-worker population totaled 55,000 . . . the *betabelero*, the Mexican sugar-beet worker, became the primary source of labor," eclipsing the Polish and Russian populations that had dominated in the 1920s (Balderrama and Rodríguez 19–20).

However, the late 1930s proved as challenging for Mexican workers as for everyone else. As reported by the *New York Times*, by 1937 "two million of the two and a half million Mexicans in the United States were out of work" (qtd. in Balderrama and Rodríguez 91). Wages for sugar-beet workers fell from twenty-eight dollars to ten dollars an acre (92). This struggle would define the Great Depression years for Mexican workers on multiple levels, with many opting for repatriation over competing for jobs with other American workers (Balderrama and Rodríguez 142).

It is therefore important that "The Gambler, the Nun, and the Radio" be understood as an inherently naturalist tale that depicts Mexicans as painfully alienated characters that are struggling to survive as beet workers/gamblers in a world that typifies the Wild West narrative. The title of the story seems to suggest such solitude, with the definite article *the* ultimately underscoring the great triumvirate of loneliness that will serve as one of the story's signature themes. However, Hemingway is quick to empower such alienated characters as well, which is perhaps one of the most overlooked aspects of the story. The shift from solitary isolation to empowerment occurs through language, when Cayetano Ruiz's alienation becomes a weapon with which to dupe the detective who, because he does not speak Spanish, must rely on the interpreter to translate for him. The interpreter, clearly on Cayetano's side from the very beginning, opts to manipulate Cayetano's statements, saying that he is telling the truth and that he may have been shot in the back while "spinning around," an apocryphal account at best (*CSS* 355). Cayetano's position of power amid great physical defeat paints him as a quintessential Hemingway hero whose eyes are as "alive as a hawk's" and who, in a resounding statement of recalcitrance, tells the interpreter to send the detective to hell in Spanish: "*Mandarlo al carajo*" (*CSS* 357). The absolute incompetence of the Montana detective is reinforced when he continues with his questions and the interpreter refuses to actually do his job. Instead of telling the detective what Cayetano says about the "poor Russian" who "started to give cries when they shoot him and he is giving cries ever since," the interpreter lies outright, thereby protecting Cayetano by claiming that Cayetano has actually answered the question: "He [Cayetano] says some fellow he doesn't know. Maybe the same fellow that shot him." Notably, the detective finally realizes he has been duped and asks Frazer, another patient in the hospital, to translate. The honest exchange that occurs between Frazer and Cayetano reveals camaraderie between the Mexican gambler and the white writer. Notably, both characters say, "Listen, amigo," and Cayetano finally seems satisfied that the translation is accurate, saying "You are of the great translators" (*CSS* 356). Frazer's ability to translate the conversation in this case parallels Hemingway's own craft at documenting the experiences of the Mexican beet-working populace in foreign and racist environments.

The racism of the American West rears its ugly head yet most notably when the detective, the interpreter, and Frazer leave Cayetano's room. The detective states pejoratively, "I wish I could talk spick," clearly indicating that he fails to understand that Spanish is a language and that he has no problem employing the offensive term. When Frazer asks him why he doesn't simply learn the language, the detective responds, "You don't have to get sore. I don't get any fun out of asking that spick questions. If I could talk spick it would be different." Hemingway satirizes the detective's absolute ignorance and bigotry when the interpreter says, "You don't need to talk Spanish . . . I am a very reliable interpreter" (*CSS* 357). Of course, the reader understands the irony of this statement and also admires the interpreter's correction at the same time vis-à-vis the detective's ignorance. It is here that Hemingway not only blatantly attacks racism and bigotry but creates multiple characters that privilege the victim over the perpetrator, even more ironic because Cayetano himself is being accused of criminal activity, while the racist interrogator is not.

In addition to Hemingway's critique of racism and bigotry, he also uses the story to satirize those who might argue in favor of an "English-only" United States. When Frazer asks the detective why he doesn't simply learn Spanish, a suggestion the detective seems to blatantly ignore, Hemingway exposes the small-mindedness of Montana while also critiquing the notion that English be the only language Americans need to learn. In this particular way, Hemingway inclusively supports bilingualism and derides monocultures that alienate a large portion of the Spanish-speaking populace. He clearly reveals the challenges that can occur when the small-minded Montana detective cannot communicate effectively due to his own bigotry and provincialism. While Hemingway is adamant in his depiction of the detective as a buffoon, he also addresses the impact that the West has had on the Mexican population. Hemingway reveals this centrally through the traumatized Latin American body, in this case Cayetano's physical manifestations. The onset of peritonitis, an inflammation of the lining of the abdomen, is juxtaposed against his "beautiful hands" and "fine face" (*CSS* 357). His is a body destroyed by small-town America and an American capitalist system that has reinforced the ideals of wealth and excess at the expense of the working body.

Notably, Sister Celia's positive view of Cayetano's body vindicates him both spiritually and ethically. She describes him as a fine patient who "always smiled. . . . He wouldn't go to confession to Father but he promised to say his prayers" (*CSS* 357). Celia's decision to pray for Cayetano and her overall treatment of him serve as a stark contrast to the detective's, suggesting that she, too, is some sort of an alienated victim in a world of corrupt investigators. This cadre includes Frazer, whose contact with the outside world is limited to a radio that only works when the hospital's X-ray machine isn't plugged in. Sister Cecilia's identification with Cayetano's alienation is revealed during a discussion with Frazer, one that seals the triumvirate as a cadre of solitary souls. When Sister Cecilia arrives to discuss her concerns with Frazer, she documents the Mexican's alienation in the hospital:

> "How's Cayetano, Sister Cecilia?" Mr. Frazer asked.
> "Oh, he's very bad."
> "Is he out of his head?"
> "No, but I'm afraid he's going to die."
> "How are you?"
> "I'm very worried about him, and do you know that absolutely no one has come to see him? He could die like a dog for all those Mexicans care. They're really dreadful." (*CSS* 359)

Cayetano Ruiz is clearly, like Frazer himself, an alienated soul in an unfamiliar environment. Yet, while Sister Cecilia is clearly altruistic, she does not necessarily shy away from staking claims about "those Mexicans" in the meantime (*CSS* 359). In this way, she is a much quieter but still identifiable voice of discrimination. When Cecilia later seems pleased that a group of Mexicans will visit Cayetano, she once again alludes to a sense of solitude and yet seems incapable of understanding that Cayetano is something beyond a Mexican. When she mentions that Cayetano will be receiving visitors, she claims, "He's going to have visitors. He can't see them yet, but they are going to come and that will make him feel better and know he's not forgotten by his own people." She then proceeds to explain that she told "that O'Brien boy" that "he's got to send some Mexicans up to see poor Cayetano" (*CSS* 360).

Of course, when the three Mexicans do come, it's clear that the community Sister Cecilia has endeavored to restore is long broken. This is first reinforced by the fact that the three Mexicans are physically quite different from one another. One is described as fat, the other as dark and small, and the third as thin. When Frazer offers them a drink, they discuss not Cayetano's health or condition at first but rather the prices of alcohol in Red Lodge, Montana, also comparing its quality to Big Timber. The Mexicans also seem much more interested in Frazer's radio than in their supposed comrade, asking about how many tubes it has and how much it costs. The irony, of course, is that Frazer then goes on to ask if the three Mexicans are friends of Cayetano's, and the "big one" answers, "No . . . We are friends of he who wounded him." Notably, when Frazer then goes on to ask if the three Mexicans can send one of Cayetano's actual friends, they answer, "He has no friends" (*CSS* 361). When Frazer asks him to explain, it's clear that Cayetano is alone because of his gambling and has been very successful as a result: "'From me,' said the smallest one, 'he won one hundred and eighty dollars. Now there is no longer one hundred and eighty dollars in the world.' 'From me,' said the thin one, 'he won two hundred and eleven dollars. Fix yourself on that figure'" (*CSS* 361).

Hemingway suggests here that the Mexican community in Montana is fragmented by its own poverty, underscored by Frazer's later note: "And now economics is an opium of the people" (*CSS* 367). The way in which the Mexican community has been fractured due to a desire for economic power during a period of great economic depression is reinforced when Frazer is corrected when he assumes Cayetano is wealthy because of his gambling. Indeed, one of the Mexicans states, "He is poorer than we . . . He has no more than the shirt on his back." The other Mexican intimates Cayetano's further demise when he states, "And that shirt is of little value now. . . . Perforated as it is." In addition, the thin Mexican's note that he is an acolyte-turned-apostate suggests an attempt to move away from his class status. When he argues that "Religion is the opium of the poor," he attests to faith as connected to a sort of ignorance that pervades the narrative, whether it be a reference to Sister Cecilia or the detective. At this stage, the value of Hemingway's story is clear: he conveys a community fractured by race and class, imploding from within—it is a case of social peritonitis as much as a bullet wound. Hemingway emphasizes the decay of Mexican solidarity as a result of such oppression when one of the Mexicans notes that the beet worker who shot Cayetano was a wonderful guitar player in a world in which there are "no good guitar players left" (*CSS* 362). The mourning of the beet worker's departure suggests the loss of Mexican culture at the expense of American values.

Toward the end of the story, information about Cayetano's paralysis intimates the challenges of social mobility as much as physical relocation. Sister Cecilia states the Cayetano is "paralyzed. One of the bullets hit the big nerve that goes down through his thigh and that leg is paralyzed. They only found it out when he got well enough so that he could move" (*CSS* 364). Clearly, although Frazer suggests that the nerve may regenerate, it appears that the Mexican community may not. This is revealed even further when it truly appears that Cayetano is more connected to Frazer than his *compadres*. As Frazer and Cayetano talk about their wounds, Cayetano reminds Frazer that it is normal to cry and yell when in pain, stating that if he had "a private room and a radio, [he] would be crying and yelling all night long" (*CSS* 365). Cayetano's intimate discussion with Frazer, presumably in Spanish, is juxtaposed against his sheer alienation from his countrymen, who don't even have names and have been "sent by the police" to visit (*CSS* 361). Cayetano's note that the beer they brought Frazer was probably bad, and Frazer's admission that it was reveals a common understanding that transcends race and class, a certain community of sufferers that eclipses Cayetano's status as a Mexican immigrant. That they both suffer from a disease of "nerves" seems to suggest this very reality. This said, while the identification and understanding between Cayetano and Frazer are Hemingway's way of bridging the gap between the Mexican community and the white writer (notably through the human experience of pain), it does not resolve the problem of a fragmented Mexican community.

Cayetano's further alienation is revealed by his love for the radio and his satirical stance on the Mexican community's traditional serenade. Pointing to his belly, he scoffs at their attempt, stating that he cannot laugh yet, proof that, "As musicians they are fatal" (*CSS* 365). This claim of a dead music that has been replaced by the radio's "Singsong Girl," "Little White Lies," and "Betty Co-Ed" represents in many ways the death of a culture in the form of new, invasive technologies vis-à-vis a fractured cultural community. Cayetano's sheer desire to win at the game of life as a Mexican immigrant has surely led to his decay. As he attests, "I am a poor idealist. I am the victim of illusions.... I am a professional gambler but I like to gamble. To really gamble. Little gambling is all crooked. For real gambling you need luck. I have no luck" (*CSS* 364). Cayetano's unlucky life—the fact that he is shot in the belly by a fellow *cabrón* who has no skill as a marksman—is a case in point, in addition to the fact that his gambling has involved little to no success. As Cayetano remarks, "I never carry a gun. With my luck, if I carried a gun I would be hanged ten times a year. I am a cheap card player only that ... When I make a sum of money I gamble and when I gamble I lose" (*CSS* 365–66). Yet when Frazer prompts him to consider, therefore, why he even plays, he states that there is a possibility that if he lives long enough, that will change, that if he ever has good luck, he will be rich. His statement, "I would enjoy being rich" reveals an investment, philosophically, in the American Dream of excess and wealth, ironic in that the story takes place a year after the 1929 stock market crash and three years before the beginning of the Great Depression. A gambler of the small towns ("then a big town, then start over again)," Cayetano Ruiz is living a migrant identity not that different from Steinbeck's migrant working-class population in many of his works (*CSS* 366). Hemingway's Latin American migrant workers in the American West, however, lead a sinister existence, one marred by oppression, dissolution, racism, and violence.

However, amid all of the dark undertones of the story, Hemingway ends with a suggestion that there are ways to heal communities that subvert authoritative landscapes. One way is, of course, through folkloric performance. As such, the Mexicans' return with their accordion and instruments reveals a turning point in the tale. In a deft narrative transition, Hemingway attests to music as opium for the Mexican population, the curative panacea for dissolution and marginalization. Notably, once the music starts, the conflict between Cayetano and the other Mexicans ceases to exist. Even more notably, music in the hospital brings together the Mexican community, as well as the rodeo rider, the carpenter, and presumably a white boy from a farm nearby:

> That night the Mexicans played the accordion and other instruments in the ward and it was cheerful and the noise of the inhalations and exhalations of the accordion, and of the bells, the traps, and the drum came down the corridor. . . . Down the corridor Mr. Frazer could hear them all laughing and merry with the music made by the Mexicans who had been sent by the police. The Mexicans were having a good time. (*CSS* 367)

The playing of "La Cucaracha," a traditional folk corrido often associated with the Mexican Revolution, suggests in fact that not only do Mexicans in the story heal their community by way of familiar song but as a result of shared politics. As Anita Brenner attests, "La Cucaracha" was a "jiggling nonsense ballad sung during times of tension and stress in the Mexican Revolution" (Castro 72). Rejoicing in the power of revolution as "an opium of the people," the thin Mexican explains that "La Cucaracha" is "a historic tune. . . . It is the tune of the real revolution" (*CSS* 367). The song chronicles a cockroach that has, like Cayetano, lost its hind leg and therefore cannot walk. An interesting replacement for the hind leg is often manifested in the lyrics "ya no puede caminar porque le falta marijuana pa' fumar [the cockroach can no longer walk because it no longer has marijuana to smoke]" (Castro 73). Of course, Frazer understands the history of the song even before the Mexicans sing it, in addition to the Mexican Revolution of 1910–20, because he previously alludes to marijuana as the opium of the people and argues later that revolution is not an opium but instead "a catharsis; an ecstasy which can only be prolonged by tyranny. The opiums are for before and after." Mr. Frazer's desire to listen to "La Cucaracha" another time, saying it is "better than the radio," suggests a certain identification with Latin America and the power of its history, as well as a desire to preserve Mexican culture, a collective community abroad, and the Spanish language (*CSS* 368).

In closing, it is easy to overlook "The Gambler, the Nun, and the Radio" as a story about the sheer universal need for an anesthetic, whether that be alcohol, religion, a radio, money, or music. However, scholars should attune to the historicity of the story as it relates to the Latin America Hemingway knew and loved. It is clear from the beginning of the tale that Hemingway's motives in writing the story are not driven solely by a need for the great triumvirate of gambler, nun, and radio. Instead, he is deeply committed to telling the stories of a Mexican community in the West and its struggles for survival amid a racist and provincial Montana, where an economic crisis has driven a wedge between the have and have-nots, a theme in the Hemingway's novel published only four years later in *To Have and Have Not*. In doing so, Hemingway depicts the struggles of Mexicans living north of the border and the challenges of maintaining a sense of community amid forces that consistently threaten their survival. In addition, through Frazer's own valuation of Mexican culture and language, Hemingway paints a hero amid a community of corrupt white racists who had a history of referring to Mexicans as "spicks." As racial profiling continues to be an issue for the Chicano and Mexican immigrant populations in America today, Hemingway's story is a refreshing reminder of the social justice issues Latin Americans face in contemporary American society. This makes the story one of Hemingway's best, one that can yield wonderful dividends for scholars who continue to explore Hemingway's Latin American imagination.

Teaching the Text

Teachers familiar with critical race theory should address Ernest Hemingway's "The Gambler, the Nun and the Radio" by encouraging students to engage in an analysis of the historical underpinnings of the 1930s in the rural Mountain West. A first means by which to do so would be reading about the politics of whiteness in the 1930s and 1940s, which spurred much of the anti-Mexican sentiment of the times, including but not limited to the immigration laws that would define the period leading up to the 1930s. Students should study, for example, the imposition of a literacy test in 1917 and the Bureau of Immigration's decision to establish the U.S. Border Patrol in 1924 (Gross 162). The repatriation to Mexico and forced deportation that defined the 1930s, a time period during which roughly half a million Mexican immigrants were repatriated to Mexico, would be critical information for students attempting to grasp a sense of the historical landscape of Hemingway's story. In addition to discussing forced and voluntary repatriation, teachers should focus significantly on the lives of

Mexicans, such as those in Hemingway's story, who remained in the country and faced significant racism and bigotry. As Ariela Gross mentions, Mexicans in the Southwest suffered Jim Crow–like segregation that characterized their daily lives as "second-class citizens" (163). Hemingway's story illuminates the degree of alienation Mexican migrants faced in the 1930s, while also documenting the realities of those who remained in the rural Mountain West after many had opted to leave. However, pedagogy should also center around critical race theory's focus on Mexican American organizations and political resistance as an extension activity after studying their segregation and alienation in states like Montana; some examples are LULAC, which formed in 1927, and AGIF (the American GI Forum), which burgeoned during the post-WWII years (Gross 165–66). Both organizations worked to address racial discrimination and aimed to uplift and galvanize Chicanos vis-à-vis the nativist and white American rhetoric they faced. Finally, teachers should also consider the importance of instructing students to employ a critical race theorist's approach when studying the plethora of court cases that defined Chicanos as white (such as *Inland Steel Co. v. Barcelona*, *In re. Rodriguez*, *Independent School District v. Salvatierra*, and *Hernandez v. State*) in order to understand the legal limitations of racism. Asking students to understand that legal definitions of whiteness did not promise or privilege greater freedoms would be pedagogically critical; George Martínez has argued a relevant point in this case: "Legal recognition of the Mexican American as white had only a slight impact on private conduct. Far from having a privileged status, Mexican Americans faced discrimination very similar to that experienced by African Americans. . . . In all these respects, actual social behavior failed to reflect the legal norms that defined Mexican Americans as white" (490). Martínez's critical race theory regarding the ironies of white legal status—and the court cases that contributed to this irony—would be invaluable terrain for students.

A final goal of any teacher who assigns Hemingway's story should situate itself in the relevance of the story in the present. Having students analyze the present-day lives of Mexican migrant workers in the Mountain West should be a central area for study. Indeed, Montana is still an attractive state for Mexican migrants due to what Leah Schmalzbauer describes as "a surge in the demand for low-wage construction workers and landscapers, a demand that has been filled in large part by Mexican migrants" (755). Between 2000 and 2005, Montana's Latino population grew by 21 percent, yet much of the racism of the 1920s and 1930s remains: "Hostile letters to the editor, service providers, employers, and educators who do not speak Spanish, the presence of white supremacist groups, and high housing costs in the region's town centers have forced this new and growing community into the social, economic, and geographic margins" (Schmalzbauer 755). These realities make Hemingway's story a particularly valuable one for teaching in the classroom, particularly at a time when racist rhetoric has pervaded and defined the political scene and the 2016 election cycle.

In closing, while scholars have taken up Hemingway's work via the study of Cuba and Spain, very little to no work has been done on Hemingway's portrayal of other Latin American countries existing in both North and South America. Moreover, Hemingway's "The Gambler, the Nun, and the Radio" has never been carefully examined as a story about the presence of Mexican migrant workers in the West. Teachers and scholars who are looking for new angles on Hemingway should take note of the story's ability to document a Mexican presence in the state during the Great Depression years and Mexicans' growing sense of alienation amid racial profiling that defined the 1930s. In addition, teachers can employ "The Gambler, the Nun, and the Radio" to incite fresh and relevant discussions about Chicano and Mexican lives today: the struggles they face and the lives they live. As a result, a closer examination of Hemingway's work reveals new directions for scholars and students in the realm of critical race theory and Chicano studies.

Teaching the Harlem Renaissance through Hemingway
Divergences and Intersections of *The New Negro* and *In Our Time*

Candice Pipes

My approach to teaching Hemingway's *In Our Time* and Locke's *The New Negro* grows out of an undergraduate junior seminar I recently led exploring the work of 1920s American authors from a multicultural, multiracial perspective. The American literary expatriates living in Paris stood as only one of the lost generations struggling to find themselves in post–World War I America. Another group, equally as literary—called the "Lost Generation Negrotarians," the title given them by David Levering Lewis via Zora Neale Hurston—was amassing in Harlem. Both groups were products of their own migrations, one out of and one in to Manhattan. Both desired to understand and heal fragmented selves in the wake of modernization: the devastating violence of war, racial injustice, the death of American romanticism and the birth of American realism, and urbanization in the wake of expanding industrialization. I submit that the surface-level accessibility and conspicuous complexity of *The New Negro* and *In Our Time* make these texts practical choices for use in the undergraduate and graduate classroom as an introduction to both black and white modernisms and as an introduction to the micro-affirmations present in Hemingway countered by the micro-inequities found in the writing of the Harlem Renaissance. Ultimately, my hope is that through this comparative study of white and black modernist literature, students will expand their definition of modernism and understand more clearly how all of these authors (and artists) have contributed to the modernist period in meaningful ways.

As students attempt to define the literary contributions of both lost generations in terms of modernism, it becomes necessary to flush out where one literary circle falls in relation to the other. Understanding modernism as a break with traditional modes of Western thought in order to provide new ways of understanding a changed world, undergraduate students reeling in their own states of transformation, identify with the emergence of a kind of liminality, a condition of in-betweenness best defined by the myriad dichotomous juxtapositions dealt with complexly in modernist art: life/death, youth/maturity, peace/war, order/chaos, pastoral/urban, etc. Rita Barnard employs Hamlin Garland's prophetic 1894 vision of modern art to describe the stimulus of modernist fiction, offering that "the emergent literature would react against the traditions of the past and attend fearlessly to the uglier contemporary aspects of reality" (40). Students explore how both American expatriate authors and Harlem Renaissance authors produced fiction fittingly described by these terms as modernist and how the underlying motivations and inspirations of each group's art helps indicate not only root commonalities but also distinctions in their respective explorations of the modern human condition. Using a framework inspired by Kirk Curnutt's model for understanding what he calls "expatriate modernism," I will show how pairing *The New Negro* and *In Our Time* will not only help students understand modernism as a consequence of the First World War, but also how modernism exists as a consequence of America's race war.

I am often surprised by the lack of knowledge college students have regarding the racial history of the United States. Therefore, I first work to give students an understanding of the racial landscape of America in the 1920s. I use 1925 as a case study. This year reflected an economic and cultural struggle between two battling anxieties: (1) a paradigm shift from a production to a consumer culture, and (2) a latent sense of a postwar America suffering from what we now know as post-traumatic stress disorder. While the casualties of war faced the inability to fully recover from the trauma of war, the hints of imminent financial devastation also began to appear.[1] We can then define 1925, a year of transition, as a year that fittingly housed complex binary oppositions that manifested themselves not only in the separate migrations of the nation's literary elite (including Fitzgerald and Dos Passos), but in unmoving racial tensions seething below the surface. Students are generally amazed to learn that in 1925 the Ku Klux Klan and Marcus Garvey's Universal Negro Improvement Association and African Communities League each boasted four million members. The nation outwardly exuded a new-found war-tested confidence but inwardly stood on the verge of implosion.

This certainty of implosion was already demonstrated by the Bloody Summer of 1919. I have students research the race riots of 1919 and we begin to make connections between this violence and literature; after all, Claude McKay's most famous poem, "If I Must Die," was written in response to these uprisings. My students learn that these race riots existed as a testament to the magma chamber of racial unrest exerting pressures on the American volcano. Responding to the extinguished flame of hope burning in the heart of an expectant black America with the return of black troops from the war in 1919 (an expectancy quenched by white supremacist economic and legal actions), Chicago, South Carolina, Mississippi, Texas, Washington, D.C., and other cities exploded into racial riots. With racial injustice rampant and lynchings approaching the numbers recorded during the post-Reconstruction era, the riots existed as black America's near impotent gesture to respond to white America "putt[ing] blacks in their place" (Douglas 87). This betrayal and accompanying tension helped create the perfect storm necessary to produce another explosion in 1925—black literature. We read Amiri Baraka's "Return of the Native" and discuss how this very real racial violence underwrites Baraka's description of Harlem as "vicious modernism. BangClash" (217). The racial landscape of 1925 was exactly that—a banging, clashing struggle for rights, for empowerment. This "BangClash" motivated authors, poets, and artists to rebel against the Negro voice as heard through translations of whiteness via minstrel shows and strong, patriarchal patronage. In fact, the label "New Negro" emerged out of this clashing and the black writers used this "violent and transforming" time to construct a new conception of blackness better armed to defend against "the alternatives of supine and humiliating submission and stimulating but hurtful counter-prejudice" (Baraka line 5; Locke 13).

Once students understand the racial dynamic of 1920s America and particularly the significance of the year 1925 as the literary witnessing to this dynamic, I spend some time introducing them to the concept of expatriate modernism. Both the American expatriate authors and the Harlem Renaissance authors produced fiction fittingly described by Alfred Kazin's understanding of modernism as "the need to learn what the reality of life was in our modern era" (qtd. in Barnard 39), but a closer examination of the underlying motivations and inspirations of each group's art helps indicate root commonalities and essential distinctions in their respective explorations of the modern human condition. Kirk Curnutt differentiates expatriate modernism from American modernism, providing a helpful framework to better understand how New Negro modernism converges and diverges with the expatriate literary movement. His project of including the expatriate literary circle within modernism while distinguishing their work with certain specific characteristics allows for insightful considerations of expatriate literary texts but fails to acknowledge the black writers of the Harlem Renaissance as similarly expatriated. We read the introduction to Curnutt's *Ernest Hemingway and the Expatriate Modernist Movement* and think about both the significance of Curnutt's omission and the usefulness of his model. Considering the Harlem Renaissance as its own type of expatriate experience—as a self-exile to Harlem from Southern racism, predominately white environments, and/or economic stagnancy—can help us better understand the intersections and diversions of New Negro modernism and expatriate literature. This is my challenge to students—how can we construct a matrix similar to Curnutt's, identifying characteristics of New Negro modernism using both fiction and visual art from *The New Negro*, that align with the five distinctions of expatriate modernism, which we examine through Hemingway's *In Our Time*?

Curnutt first claims that expatriate modernism "depicts displacement as a fundamental condition of life in the early 20th century" (12). In this same sense, Ann Douglas refers to the expatriate writers as "orphans" (27). The feeling of dislocation, albeit voluntary, gives rise to stories of failed and impossible homecomings, stories rooted in the authors' being "homesick for certainties of childhood," but unable to return home as home has forever changed (Cowley 9). Rita Barnard, using the title of an *In Our Time* story, calls this the "condition of being 'out of season,'" a condition Clinton Burhans imagines as a world in which "everything man expects or wants or seeks collapses when he reaches for it" (56, 99). I point students to Hemingway's story "Soldier's Home" to best exemplify this condition. Krebs returns home from the war late to a town saturated with war stories and a family both concerned and uninterested in him as he struggles to find his place in a world forever changed. Krebs is disillusioned but, as Burhans points out, "less by the war than by the normal peacetime world" (97). Krebs has learned in the war that the worst offense is lying—an offense with devastating consequences—a lesson that quickly turns into a dilemma as Krebs realizes that "to be listened to at all he had to lie" ("Soldier's Home" 69). Unwilling to suffer the consequences of lying, recognizing that "it wasn't worth it," Krebs, with stark honesty, tells his mother he does not love her and learns another lesson—the same rules do not apply at war and at home. Krebs's honesty causes his mother injury, presumably the very consequence Krebs so desperately attempts to escape. Ultimately, Krebs decides to depart home—"he would go to Kansas City and get a job" (77)—and the story ends leaving Krebs effectively homeless. Krebs's self-exile mirrors that of American expatriates, and Hemingway's refusal to provide a resolution for Krebs's feeling of displacement suggests the modern human condition of being an orphan is a terminal one.

I then ask students to think about how we can consider *The New Negro* in the context of Curnutt's first characteristic. Students note that the New Negro modernists are not so much expressing displacement, but instead depicting Harlem as the city of refuge—making Harlem the black orphanage. Ann Douglas explains, "[I]f white moderns thought of themselves as orphans, the black moderns, whose ancestors were kidnapped from their native land and sold into slavery in an alien country, were in fact, America's only true orphaned group" (83). We read Rudolph Fisher's story "The City of Refuge" and consider "the impulse of the first literary generations . . . to regard Harlem as a trope" (de Jongh 15). To Fisher's credit, although he participates in the early myth making of Harlem, he challenges the myth by also presenting Harlem as the city of refuse.

The story's protagonist, King Solomon Gillis, flees to Harlem after shooting a white man in North Carolina. Naïve and overwhelmed by spectacles like black policemen, Gillis gets hoodwinked into a drug operation and is eventually arrested. At first resisting the arrest, Gillis finally relaxes and grins when a black cop enters to help detain him. An ending that de Jongh argues holds Harlem "true to its symbolic promise" (18). Fisher, however, subversively spears the mythology of Harlem by juxtaposing refuge and refuse through his own imagery. The beginning of the story contrasts stifling "heat, oppression, suffocation" with "Clean air, blue sky, bright sunlight" (57). Fisher describes Harlem in one breath as "the land of plenty . . . also the city of refuge" and in another as a "sewer of sounds and smells" (58). Fisher's story acknowledges the importance of Harlem as the figurative orphanage for an abandoned people, but also refuses to fully romanticize its power. Ultimately, in order for young Gillis to escape the fate of lynching, he must accept the less damaging fate of jail. Fisher suggests Harlem provides opportunities for black Americans (albeit not all good), and that uplift is a process of degrees of better fates.

The second distinction of expatriate modernist writers my students and I explore is their need to "denounce America as a land of repressive morality where puritanical attitudes render the nation incapable of acknowledging the uncertainties of the age" (Curnutt 13). Hemingway attempts this by exposing the "world and human condition with masks off, with all fraudulent illusion stripped away" (Burhans 91). We read "Mr. and Mrs. Elliot," both as a critique of traditional Victorian modes of heterosexual romance and as a humorous lance at the expatriate literary circle (namely the Elliots). The story depicts the changing sexual landscape by mocking a "bit of leftover Victorian sexual moralism." Mr. and Mrs. Elliot marry after a traditional courtship; Mr. Elliot "wanted to keep himself pure so that he could bring to his wife the same purity of mind and body he expected for her" ("Mr. and Mrs. Elliot" 68, 85). Ironically, the only woman Mr. Elliot can catch with this lure is a much older spinster, a reality that concedes "that prudery is the product of another time" (Stewart 69). The couple attempts to conceive several times in and outside of America, but Mr. Elliot's impotence combined with Mrs. Elliot's sterility exist as a "metaphor for barrenness in the relationship," and the marriage progresses badly until Mrs. Elliot's lover arrives: "Mrs. Elliot became much brighter after her girl friend came" (Curnutt 89; Hemingway 87). Hemingway privileges the nontraditional lesbian relationship and hints at Mr. Elliot's homosexuality. The couple's circumstance exists as a commentary against relapsing Puritanism in American with Prohibition existing as one symptom. Matthew Stewart suggests that Hemingway's observations are more complex than that, arguing that the story really critiques the fakeness of the expatriate circle and their "overprivileged dilettantism" (69). Viewed in this light, the students recognize that the story becomes Hemingway's denouncement of his friends' denouncements as shams—an uncloseting of his community's own regressive morality in hopes of encouraging a truer liberalism.

Again, I ask students to think of *The New Negro* in the context of repressive morality and Puritanical values. My students conclude that for black writers, racial oppression trumps sexual repression; hence, the New Negro modernists denounce America as a land of oppression, where racist policies render the nation incapable of acknowledging African Americans as human beings. The oft-quoted W. E. B. Du Bois assertion in 1903 that "the problem of the twentieth century is the problem of the color line" articulates the necessity and urgency that African American artists felt to confront this problem. The New Negroes were, in fact, asserting an anti-racist platform, overtly rejecting racial oppression and injustice and, in doing so, producing a culture reflecting these initiatives. The creation of an Afro-American culture, in the sense that culture exists as something uniquely human, was critical to combating racist ideologies that separate whites as human beings and blacks as sub-persons. Not surprisingly, then, the self-awareness exhibited within a newly forming ideology of blackness did, in fact, denounce American racial oppression—it had to. We study Claude McKay's poem "White Houses" as one example of how this denouncement was accomplished through literature.

Alain Locke in his foreword to *The New Negro* victoriously and ironically asserts, "we shall let the Negro speak for himself" as the fundamental premise of the anthology (xxv). So it is no surprise that Claude McKay was irate when Locke changed the name of his poem "The White House" to "White Houses" for the publication. Uncomfortable with the radical nature of the overt attack on the president, Locke opted for a more subversive rather than assertive title. McKay's poem, however, successfully strikes (albeit more generally than desired) by beginning with a pointed use of second person, "Your door is shut against my tightened face" (1). Subversively using a Shakespearean sonnet, McKay converts the traditional love poem into one seething with anger and revenge, what Baker cites as "the denigration of form—a necessary ('forced,' as it were) adoption of the standard that results in an effective blackening" (85). McKay reveals his strength: "But I possess the courage and the grace / To bear my anger proudly and unbent" and his intention to combat his disenfranchisement, "Oh I must keep my heart inviolate / Against the potent poison of your hate" (lines 3–4, 13–14). By exposing the hate felt as a result of the opposing "you," McKay demonizes the enemy while ennobling himself and in effect molests the pristine quality of these white houses. Despite Locke's attempts to defuse the poem's potency, McKay effectively renounces, via the image of the white house, its symbolic political and legal oppression and its gestation of white privilege that actively feeds on the oppression of black Americans.

The third distinction we consider is that the expatriates "did not renounce their nationality. Rather, they regarded Paris as a foreign realm in which they could create new identities, craft new values, and explore unconventional and taboo behaviors" (Curnutt 13). The result of rejecting repression is a newfound freedom to be oneself and to question tradition, authority, and truth. As a consequence of the war, one must reconcile between split selves and competing binary positions—conservative/liberal, progressive/regressive, lawful/unlawful—before any new identity can be formed. Hemingway's short story "Out of Season" presents a couple in the process of sorting through the dichotomous nature of modernism. Tourists abroad, the husband and wife hire a drunken townsman to take them fishing even though fishing is out of season. The wife, cold and hostile to her husband, does not want to go—"we're probably being followed by the game police now," she says—but continues anyway (*IOT* 100). The husband seems up for the excitement but is relieved when fishing is not possible, the law remains unbroken, and the sun comes out to reveal the "wonderful day" (102). Torn between competing identities and the risk that role-playing a new identity inherently presents, the couple survives with ambiguous results. Michael Stewart suggests the underlying issue is abortion. The pregnant wife desires "no part in either 'operation,'" while the husband, not ready for the responsibility of fatherhood, moves toward unlawful termination (73). In this sense, we can read the story as a happy ending, with no law broken. The happy ending reading ironically, then, staunchly roots "Out of Season" in conventionality and tradition. Significantly, Curnutt does not require that expatriate modernism change conventionality, just that it explore unconventionality as "Out of Season" undeniably does.

Students discover that while the expatriates challenged conventionality but did not renounce their nationality, the black modernists, having had their nationality renounced for them, searched for an identifying cultural location and found ancestral art. Although there existed significant Pan-Africanist movements, some with desires to renounce American national allegiance, many of the New Negro modernists worked to create a new cultural identity by reaching back to African art and primitivist influences. The significance of Locke's inclusion of graphic art in his project, Baker submits, is that it "produce[d] an *interpretation* of the Afro-American unlike any" yet seen (71). The preeminent example of this combination of African and primitive art with modernist style in *The New Negro* is the artwork of Aaron Douglas. Arriving in Harlem just months before the anthology's publication, Douglas wrote to Locke, "[W]e must let down our buckets into our own souls where joy and pain, mirth and sadness, still flows swift and deep and free, and drink until we are drunk as with an overpowering desire for expression" (Kirschke 31). Douglas, infused with new possibility and a new subject (blacks), became known as "the father of Black American art" (Kirschke 26).

Amy Helene Kirschke, one of the few and the preeminent scholar on Aaron Douglas praises Douglas's importance as the "first African American artist to explore modernism and to incorporate African art into his work" (xiii). Douglas's work, also symptomatic of aforementioned bifurcations, severely contrasted black and white, "vacillat[ing] between advocating separatism and integration" (Kirschke xiii). Douglas's work, reflective of his mentor and teacher, German artist Winold Reiss, combines African ancestral art and industrial modernity—an amalgamation of African masks and skyscrapers, tribal dance, and smokestacks. Kirschke reveals that Douglas's reliance on primitivism reflects not a desire to return to Africa, but an aspiration to create a new African American art form; Douglas "accepted some of the ideas of primitivism, but argued that it allowed American blacks to make a unique contribution" (46). Douglas viewed African art as a "source of inspiration, not an escape" (Kirschke 47). Douglas's drawing "Rebirth" tackles the ideology of the New Negro being reborn from the Old. A large sun shines its rays down from the left corner, illuminating the chaos of the world below. A world confused in the midst of stand-alone open eyes indicates the New Negro's wide-open outlook for a better future. From the top right corner, a black face casts a panoptic gaze on the flailing and burdened bended-kneed bodies in the center of the picture, surrounded by sharp edges and menacing African masks. The middle of the picture is tunneled, representing the birth canal. Douglas ultimately suggests that rebirth, the creation of a new identity, is a traumatic process of swimming through the past in order to achieve the present.

The fourth distinction of expatriate modernists we pursue is their intense desire to "explore the consequences of World War I, depicting it as a major cause of their disillusionment and disaffection" (Curnutt 17). Combining his own journalistic experience and what Ann Douglas calls "terrible honesty," Hemingway uses inter-chapters, or vignettes, to explore war, its consequences, and the resulting disillusionment. Hemingway is famous, in part, due to his iceberg approach to writing, and this technique is never more apparent than in the vignettes, which act as inter-chapters between short stories in *In Our Time*. I ask students to consider the purpose and effect of these vignettes as central to Hemingway's project. Jackson Benson describes these vignettes as the "attempt to express the impact of the world on a newspaperman who has had the opportunity to see something of that world, and to express that impact as 'impression rather than as 'report'" (106). Initially critiqued as a source of disunity in the text, the vignettes, according to Burhans, are where "Hemingway places violence and death on which man imposes order and meaning at the center of a world of chaotic disorder and violence, thus implying subtly from the first (bullfighting) he can learn something about the second (the world) and how to live in it" (90). Hemingway explores the ways men in war, faced with death, wounded psychologically and physically, respond differently. One soldier resorts to convenient faith, "Dear jesus please get me out. Christ please please please Christ. If you'll only keep me from getting killed I'll do anything you say. I believe in you and I'll tell every one in the world that you are the only one that matters" (*IOT* 67). The soldier survives and does not keep his promise. Alternatively, Hemingway offers an injured Nick's response, "You and me we've made a separate peace" (63). Many read this scene as evidence that Nick deserts from the war—no longer a willing participant—to fish the river alone, he and his comrade Rinaldi now "not patriots" (63). In other vignettes, Hemingway juxtaposes the controlled violence of bullfighting with the chaotic violence of war. David Leigh reads the bullring as a contrast to "the lost world of the expatriate, where the smoke of dead ideals blinds all to any hope for achievement and self-realization" (132). Hemingway does champion the honorable characteristics of "courage, responsibility, determination, skill, and grace" over those demonstrating a lack—"incompetence, fear, drunkenness, evasion" (Burhans 92). Significantly, my students point out that in the end the celebrated bullfighter Maera dies, "his head on his arms, his face in the sand" (31). Death, the consequence of even the best planned war, remains inevitable.

With some thought, students notice that the New Negro modernists focus less on the consequences of World War I, but more on the consequences of slavery and the failed efforts of Reconstruction as a source of their disillusionment and fragmentation. Summers suggests that one New Negro modernist, Claude McKay, "experienced the growing movement of disillusion that was at the heart of European artistic and intellectual circles immediately following the war," albeit for different reasons (251). Ann Douglas discloses that there was no black novel of the war, claiming "evidence suggests that for black writers the Great War did not emblematize modernity" and stating that "the Negro's disillusion with the war focused on the racial injustice it exemplified and furthered, rather than on the disturbing and violent realities that the war's new technologies had laid bare" (88–89). World War I is starkly absent from the pages of *The New Negro* while almost every text conveys, whether implicitly or explicitly, the horrors of slavery and the unfulfilled promises of Reconstruction.

The New Negro modernists, too, suffered from PTSD, but the catalyst was one that stemmed back centuries versus a single decade. I ask my students to find the texts that best demonstrate how these authors battle through the psychological dissonance of a trauma that is at once collective and yet not wholly shared. In "Song of the Sun," Jean Toomer petitions to save the Negro spirituals—the source of strength for so many during the terror of slavery: "One plum was saved for me, one seed becomes / An everlasting song, a singing tree, / Caroling softly souls of slavery, / What they were, and what they are to me, / Caroling softly souls of slavery"—showing how the purpose served in slavery is still required in the present (lines 19–23). Langston Hughes explores the shame of slavery and Jim Crow legislation in "I, Too," asserting part ownership of America and infusing hope in black America that "they'll see how beautiful I am / And be ashamed—" (15–16). Acknowledging that the concept of "black beauty" is a foreign one, in part due to the grotesque imaginings of blackness taking place in popular blackface minstrelsy, Hughes celebrates the dignity enacted daily by black performers in another poem, "Minstrel Man": "Because my mouth / is wide with laughter, / You do not hear / My inner cry, / Because my feet / Are gay with dancing, / You do not know / I die" (9–16).

Hughes is able to identify the pain in the micro-inequities of white stereotyping of blacks and simultaneously restore dignity and pride to the black body. The New Negro modernists' lack of attention to World War I was not meant to diminish its tragedies or discount its significance in the lives of blacks, but rather to elucidate the ongoing war still waging in the black community.

Lastly, we discuss Curnutt's fifth characteristic of expatriate modernism, that this movement was a "youth culture movement . . . in a world in which adulthood seemed an initiation into little more than hypocrisy and deceit, growing up for them signaled a fall from innocence into moral corruption" (19). Ann Douglas quotes Hemingway as saying, "I am in competition with the clock which keeps ticking" (39). While certainly echoing Cowley's understanding of the expatriates as "homesick for certainties of childhood" (9), we've already determined the impossibility of such homecomings. So the expatriates' search for youth surfaces as a combination of revolution and nostalgia. To grow up means to encounter the world as it is in our time—"a puzzling place in which beauty and wonder, love and compassion, are strangely mixed with cruelty and violence, suffering, loss, alienation, and death" (Burhans 97). To grow up means to accept responsibility—a struggle Hemingway faced in his own life and is evident in his story "Cross Country Snow."

"Cross Country Snow" reunites Nick with his old friend George on a ski trip in the Alps. The freedom of youth, symbolized through the swift, adrenaline-rushing skiing and male camaraderie, is contrasted with the unseen elements in the now-adult men's lives—for Nick the prison of marriage and further entrapment of impending fatherhood. Discussing the rigors of adult life, George asks, "It's hell, isn't it?," to which Nick responds, "No. Not exactly" (111). Split between competing loyalties—reminiscences of his youth and the reality of manhood—Nick's response indicates confusion and, to an extent, resignation. Michael Stewart adeptly comments on this scene: "the 'not exactly' bespeaks two things. In part it expresses normal misgivings about beginning any new stage of life, especially one that brings the uncertainties and responsibilities of fatherhood, and in part indicates Nick's last vestiges of adolescence" (79). Despite outspoken desires of these two men to "just bum together," life proceeds and Nick accepts his grown=up fate, refusing to promise George another brief remission from responsibility, "there isn't any good in promising" (112). Like Nick, the expatriates' desire to reside in an adolescent state of abandon and carelessness does not mean they failed to acknowledge the futility of such thoughts.

My students quickly determine that New Negro modernism also existed as a youth movement, but in a different sense from the expatriate modernism

Kirk Curnutt offers. The African American literary elite actively recruited young minds to serve as leaders of a new generation of Negro art and ideology. In fact, Alain Locke dedicates *The New Negro* to "the Younger Generation" quoting a traditional hymn, "O, rise, shine for thy Light is a'coming" (xii). The movement was a success primarily due to persons like Alain Locke and Charles Johnson working as literary agents to promote the Harlem Renaissances as a "political strategy" (Ann Douglas 303). David Levering Lewis discusses the weight of these influences, commenting that "markets, exposure, education, intercultural exchange—these were Johnson's goals, goals in which notions of art for its own sake hardly played a part" (97). Whether art for art's sake played a part or not, in less than a decade twenty novels were produced by the Harlem Renaissance, all standing on the shoulders of *The New Negro*'s publication in 1925 (de Jongh 34).

Alain Locke even dedicates one of his essays in *The New Negro* to youth. In the "Negro Youth Speaks," Locke writes, "Youth speaks, and the voice of the New Negro is heard. What stirs inarticulately in the masses is already vocal upon the lips of the talented few, and the future listens, however the present may shut its ears" (47). Understanding that the future of the race lies in the hands of his chosen, Locke positions the young black poets (Hughes, McKay, Cullen) as the lighthouses meant to guide a lost generation through the fog of modernity. Echoing Hughes's concern with the minstrel-like depictions of blackness prevalent in American culture, Locke offers that this new generation of black poets (while subtly taking a jab at older ones, namely Paul Laurence Dunbar), "have shaken themselves free from the minstrel tradition and the fowling-nets of dialect, and through acquiring ease and simplicity in serious expression, have carried the fake-gift to the altitudes of art" (48). The new face of blackness exists, no longer a caricatured contortion of blackness, but a realistic rendering as the picture titled "Young Negro" placed immediately before Locke's essay suggests. Offering art as "an emancipating vision to America," Locke offers up a new, younger generation of black artists lost, but trying to be found, and resolutely places them at once in harmony and in conflict with their white modernist counterparts (53).

Ultimately, my students come to several conclusions by the end of this comparative literary experiment: (1) They tend to reject traditional scholarship that diminishes or minimizes the role of black writers in the modernist movement, (2) They understand clearly the influence Hemingway and other expatriate modernists had on the modernist movement and the writers of the Harlem Renaissance, and (3) They are able to articulate how the New Negro and expatriate modernists are both similar and distinct in their respective projects. Unequivocally, the shared sentiment of loss defined both the expatriate literary elite of Paris and the African American pioneers of Harlem as they attempted to comprehend the modern human condition. The year 1925 stands out as the beginning of two considerable components to the modernist era—the introduction of Hemingway to America and the announcement of the Harlem Renaissance. Uprooted by wars on both fronts, Hemingway and African American authors unearthed injustice, hypocrisy, and suffering in the ways they best could—by offering the truth as they saw it, no longer hidden underneath piles of sentimentality or distorted in grotesque caricature. Ultimately, Hemingway and his circle of expatriate friends and the young African American authors of the Harlem Renaissance suffered as orphans, terminally out of place, and sought solace and healing through their writing—not only for themselves, but for their modern world.

Note

1. Two novels published in 1925 nicely juxtapose these anxieties: Fitzgerald's *The Great Gatsby* and Dos Passos's *Manhattan Transfer*. Rooted deeply in the mythology of the American dream, the novels explore how the promise of "making it big" is compromised by portraits of devastating failure. The desire for upward mobility within the complexity of the modern age upsets the American dream's seeming simplicity.

Lost in Transition

Questions of Belonging in Hemingway's "Soldier's Home" and Hughes's "Home"

Joshua M. Murray

In his 1956 autobiography, *I Wonder as I Wander,* Langston Hughes includes a chapter titled "A Hemingway Story." Here, he discusses his time spent in Spain in 1937 when he met many white American writers whom he had not previously known while still in the United States. As the title suggests, the chapter ultimately focuses on his interactions with Ernest Hemingway, whom Hughes labeled "the most celebrated American in Spain" and "a big likable fellow" (363). During their brief time together, Hughes appears to have gained a strong respect for Hemingway, both as a person and as a writer. Hughes demonstrates this admiration through his retelling of a scene that occurred at a bar in Spain, an incident that Hemingway later recycled as the basis for his short story "The Butterfly and the Tank." In considering the way in which Hemingway composed the fictional tale around the true story, Hughes wrote, "In many of my stories I have used real situations and actual people as a starting point, but have tried to change and disguise them so that in fiction they would not be recognizable. I was interested in observing what Hemingway did to real people in his story, some of whom he described almost photographically" (365). This selection from Hughes's autobiography provides an interesting backstory for one of Hemingway's stories, while also giving insight into his writing strategy. Others, including James Plath, Kenneth G. Johnston, and Mark P. Ott, have examined Hughes's report of the story's origin. Yet more significant than Hughes's insider information is the intersection of these two writers in Spain. In 1937, when Hemingway and Hughes had each published several books and received numerous accolades, these two authors arguably represented the upper echelon of American literature. In this way, white and black literary circles overlapped to a degree that demands attention.

Twelve years prior to his Spanish introduction to Hughes, Hemingway published the debut short story collection that put him on the literary radar. *In Our Time* (1925) provided Americans with their initial glimpse of his writerly prowess. Comprised of short stories intermingled with brief vignettes, this collection introduced readers to the recurring themes of war, fishing, and bullfighting. One specific story, "Soldier's Home," tells the story of a young man's return from Europe following World War I and his difficulty readjusting to American society. On its own, this story transcends time and creates an easily relatable tale. Apparently, Hughes thought the same thing, as his story "Home," published nine years later, shares similarities that warrant closer analysis. In the introduction to their volume *Hemingway and the Black Renaissance* (2012), editors Gary Edward Holcomb and Charles Scruggs briefly discuss the connection between these two stories, contending that Hughes "effectively idolized" and "expressed his admiration for Hemingway by rewriting his brilliant short story" (10). Indeed, each piece follows a protagonist's transatlantic journey from Europe to America and the subsequent sense of dislocation that occurs when attempting to settle back into hometown life. While there appears to be a definite relation between the two stories, my goal here is not to ascertain Hughes's motivations and goals in appropriating Hemingway's plot. Rather, I hope to demonstrate the valuable pedagogical tool that can arise from a purposeful juxtaposition of the two stories.

Regardless of the similarities I hope to highlight here, the short stories nonetheless exhibit distinct settings and themes all their own. The protagonists approach their individual conflicts from opposite sides of the color line, and the language of each story underscores Hemingway's minimalism and Hughes's poetic style. In spite of these differences, however, the parallel plots shine through. Hemingway's "Soldier's Home" details the story of Harold Krebs, a young soldier who has recently returned to his Oklahoma hometown following the Great War. Once home, Krebs fails to meet his family's expectations for marriage and a career, instead exhibiting ennui and a lack of motivation. Perhaps not surprisingly, Krebs has difficulty readapting to civilian life, and he frequently wishes he could return to Europe. Hughes's "Home," published in *Esquire* and as part of his short story collection *The Ways of White Folks*, both in 1934, maintains a similar plotline and trajectory, though the deviations emphasize the racial difference in the two protagonists. In this iteration, the narrative follows Roy Williams, an African American violinist. Like Krebs, Roy has spent several years abroad in Europe, though he gains this experience as part of an international music troupe rather than as part of a military regiment. Just like Krebs, Roy finds his return to America lacking, as it displays none of the homely characteristics one might expect. As the result of a mere latitudinal move, Roy can no longer enjoy many of the freedoms he took for granted in Paris and Berlin, solely because of his skin color. The more time Roy spends in Missouri, the more he becomes disillusioned with any sense of nostalgia he once held. Unlike Krebs's situation in which he must live with a postwar depression, however, Roy's story ends more tragically. When the racist citizens of Roy's hometown feel intimidated, they incite a riot and ultimately lynch him. In this way, Hughes's tale drastically deviates from the formula of Hemingway's.

Teaching these two stories alongside one another can therefore pave the way for a multifaceted classroom discussion. When presenting these stories to my students, I divide the discussion points into three main categories: transnationalism, trauma, and race. Before jumping into these concepts, however, I introduce the stories by encouraging an examination of the connection between the two authors. As I detailed earlier, Hughes admits his admiration for Hemingway's writing style in his autobiography *I Wonder as I Wander*. When looking at these two stories in tandem, then, one can see a clear link between the two. However, Hughes does not merely take the outline of Hemingway's story and "color" it, shifting the protagonist from white to black. Instead, the resulting story forms a nuanced variation of the original. While the three chronological components of the pieces—beginning, middle, and end—follow the same progression, the characters' outcomes remain irreconcilable. Nonetheless, as the basic plotline of "Home" so closely mirrors that of "Soldier's Home," the disparate endings form a complex statement worth exploring.

At the outset of their respective stories, both Harold Krebs and Roy Williams undergo a transatlantic move from Europe to the United States. As we soon learn, the time abroad forms lasting memories for the two men, creating a new standard by which they compare all future experiences. In this way, we can see how Krebs and Roy endure a sense of loss during the transition from the progressive Europe to the regressive United States. Following their travels, the protagonists reflect on their European trips, recalling the distinct differences between the cosmopolitan continent and their respective hometowns. Holcomb and Scruggs aptly explain how the shared transnational return differs for the two men: "Krebs from the war, and Roy from a Europe of culture to the war at home. Both men cannot adjust to 'home,' though the consequences for Roy are deadly, while Krebs can move to Kansas City" (11). As they point out, this transition from one side of the Atlantic to the other connects the two characters, yet their experiences and mental states back at home fully unite them.

Resulting from these transnational moves, dislocation plays a key role in the link between Krebs and Roy, yet they do not hold sole agency for it. In fact, each character's conflict appears when their American destinations—the places that should provide dependable and unconditional acceptance—reject them immediately. Each protagonist receives a less-than-warm welcome when returning to the United States. Krebs chose to stay in Europe following the conclusion of the war, not returning to Oklahoma until mid-1919. As a result, when he does finally arrive back in America, "the greeting of heroes was over. He came back much too late. The men from the town who had been drafted had all been welcomed elaborately on their return. There had been a great deal of hysteria. Now the reaction had set in. People seemed to think it was rather ridiculous for Krebs to be getting back so late, years after the war was over" (111). Frederick J. Hoffman encapsulates Krebs's state of mind succinctly when he describes him as "hurt, ill at ease, uncertain of his future, 'disenchanted'" (98). In this way, Krebs quickly figures as Other. Roy's return from his six-year stint across the Atlantic evokes a similar reaction, this time due to race. When Roy arrives off the train and announces he has come home to see his mother, one white man offers his opinion: "I hope she's gladder to see yuh than we are" (39). In the same scene, Roy slowly comes to terms with the racism that he had forgotten while outside the United States. When a man mutters a racial slur, Roy's "skin burned. For the first time in half a dozen years he felt his color. He was home" (39). The biting irony of the last sentence epitomizes the realization of both men. In this shared canon of Hemingway and Hughes, home appears as a shadow of its former self, this time characterized by unacceptance, rejection, and violence.

Therefore, in each case the titular "home" houses no sense of belonging and instead presents more hostility than hospitality. Krebs feels the pressure from his family and the surrounding community to conform to societal expectations. Now that he has returned from the war, his civil duty is to start his career, marry, and begin striving toward the capitalistic American Dream. In the traditional Hemingway fashion, "Soldier's Home" does not provide a detailed account of Krebs's experiences with war. His actions back in Oklahoma, however, do convey the sense of loss and aimlessness he feels following his return. In a historically based article, Steven Trout creates an insightful and exhaustive record detailing the extent to which soldiers had difficulty reentering American society following their enlistment in World War I. Parsing out the details of Krebs's service record, he succeeds in establishing the untold history of the young soldier. After considering the various clues within the text concerning Krebs's credentials, Trout surmises that "Krebs's war experience, unlike that of the vast majority of men who entered the U.S. Army in 1917 or 1918 (half of whom never left the United States), would have been one of unimaginable ferocity" (15). In turn, "the humiliations that attend Krebs's homecoming, his discovery that he is forgotten by his community . . . and still regarded as an adolescent by his insensitive parents, result in part from a kind of willful amnesia that permeated American culture in the 1920s—with disastrous economic and psychological results for many veterans" (16). In light of this information, it makes sense that in the flux of leaving for the war and returning from it, Krebs has traumatically lost his identity, one that had been solidly grounded in an ideological American patriotism.

Roy's trauma and disillusionment arrive more gradually, as a series of disappointments. In fact, he initially leaves Europe as a result of his realization of its shortcomings. Though he does not witness racism there to the same degree as in America, he sees intense scenes of hunger and poverty firsthand. Over time, this impacts his ability to enjoy his successful career as a musician, wherein "the glittering curtains of Roy's jazz were lined with death" (37). The inequality so affects him that it leads to a hemorrhage from which he never fully recovers. From that point onward, he must live with the "feeling that he was going to die. The cough stayed, and the sadness. So he came home to see his mother" (38). When finally back in Missouri, he attempts to continue the life he lived abroad, yet he continually encounters resistance. His reception at the train station reintroduces him to the attitudes of racist whites, and the invitation he receives to perform at the local white high school leads to increased suspicion from the townspeople. Emphasizing Roy's status as musician, Stephen Cooper posits that Hughes's short story "is about how racism and philistinism crush artistic expression and freedom" (89). Indeed, if Krebs's dissatisfaction with American societal strictures stems from his inability to reconcile a conspicuous materialism with his military experiences in Europe, then Roy's tragedy unfolds as a result of the persistent obstacles he encounters when attempting to live in America the same way he lived in Europe. Roy's premonition of death is correct, yet ironically it results not from his sickness but from his encroachment upon the racist ideology of others.

Ultimately, despite the connections between the two stories, they conclude in drastically different fashions. The persistent friction of the hostile home forces a change. Neither Krebs nor Roy can remain in their current location without some form of further transition or alteration. As Krebs's conflict reaches its climax, he maintains the agency and freedom to choose his response. While his mental dissatisfaction should not be taken lightly, as something that could be categorized as post-traumatic stress disorder in the twenty-first century, his racial identity paired with the internal status of his conflict grants him the ability to attempt a resolution through a geographical relocation. Following his mother's pleas for normalcy, Krebs decides to "go to Kansas City and get a job and she would feel all right about it" (116). Though we do not know his eventual outcome, we know there is at least a possibility for improvement or resolution.

In Roy's case, simple removal is not an option. Just as his tale is one of gradually mounting tension, his horrific death scene follows the same progression. Emphasizing the groundless nature of racist violence, Hughes effectively conveys the escalation and embellishment of Roy's crime:

> The movies had just let out and the crowd, passing by and seeing, objected to a Negro talking to a white woman—insulting a White Woman—attacking a WHITE woman—RAPING A WHITE WOMAN. They saw Roy remove his gloves and bow. When Miss Reese screamed after Roy had been struck, they were sure he had been making love to her. And before the story got beyond the rim of the crowd, Roy had been trying to rape her, right there on the main street in front of the brightly-lighted windows of the drug store. Yes, he did, too! Yes, sir! (45)

In this way, as in many other related works of the same period, the racist mob does not seek justice or truth; instead, they merely seek the chance to eliminate a man who does not fit within their paradigm. As Hans Ostrom insightfully elucidates in *Langston Hughes: A Study of the Short Fiction* (1993), "Hughes demonstrates the way in which racism is projection: Williams' lynchers do not see him; they see only the objectified 'Negro' in their minds" (52). In other words, both stories contain the same components: transnational travel, failure to readapt to American society, and continued rejection and negation. The key distinction between the two, then, appears in the racial identities of the men.

These discussion topics provide a strong starting point for a pedagogical engagement with the two short stories. Regardless of the original publication dates, the themes at play in Hemingway's and Hughes's writings ring true in our contemporary social climate where military conflict and racial violence appear in the news on a daily basis. With this in mind, I have found that the texts work well when placed together in the literature classroom. If there is the possibility for teaching the stories over two class periods, an alternative (or additional) approach to consider when creating lesson plans is the possibility of assigning "Soldier's Home" to half of the class and "Home" to the other half for the first day and then having the students switch for the second day. A fruitful in-class exercise on the first day would be to begin by asking the entire class for a list of concepts central to the stories. Presumably, this initial list would shed light on the shared characteristics of the stories, with one outlier—race—only mentioned in relation to Hughes's work. Whereas the majority of the first class period would be used for summary, the second period would allow for more in-depth discussion as to the significance of each protagonist's personal trauma and sense of homelessness, while also addressing how the addition of race further complicates the plot(s). These are only a few ideas for classroom practices, yet they offer possible entries into an important connection between authors.

In the end, one might question just how connected these two stories truly are. While it seems Hughes consciously employed Hemingway's "Soldier's Home" as the blueprint for his own "Home," the latter work is much more than a mere refiguring of the story. Instead, Hughes uses the same themes of transition and belonging to demonstrate how race alters the storyline and definitively moves it from drama to tragedy. Both exhibit similar qualities of introspection and loneliness, but Roy's experience becomes increasingly violent due to racism's removal of his agency. The resulting classroom discussion provides an opportunity for a nuanced understanding of the frequently romanticized period of American modernism. Through a purposeful juxtaposition of Hemingway and Hughes, students can also realize the extent to which the racialized American literary circles are not as separate as they may appear.

A Classroom Approach to Black Presence in *The Sun Also Rises*

Gary Edward Holcomb

The Sun Also Rises is crucial reading for courses in American modernism, American novel, and other curricula focused on the twentieth-century novel. Characterized by the novel's portrayal of the Jazz Age sexual revolution and gender-role upheaval, Hemingway's novel stages the historic shift in consciousness following the Great War, the generational rift illustrated by the "lost generation," a term attributed to Gertrude Stein in the front matter. The text is essential reading, moreover, owing to its portrayal of the interwar feeling of futility and social alienation under bourgeois capitalism. Hemingway's novel poses that the predicament of the Lost Generation—pointless existence in the early twentieth-century wasteland—may find momentary relief, an existential, transitory release from modern social convention through an engagement with what modernists thought of as primitive cultures (in this case, Basque culture) that still make meaning through premodern ritual. Yet when racial aspects of the narrative are brought to the fore, the novel poses certain difficulties for the contemporary student reader. My view is that not only should such features be foregrounded, but that these aspects are essential to teaching *The Sun Also Rises* in the contemporary classroom, shaped, rightly, by multicultural pedagogies.

The purpose of this essay is to offer a pedagogical approach that focuses on the two minor African American characters who emerge in the narrative, both seeming to verge on negligible, and both characterized through white supremacist language. The first appears in the form of the "nigger" drummer who plays at the Montmartre *bal musette*, Zelli's. The drummer is an ostensibly inconsequential character who appears in the form of Jazz Age minstrelsy, his presence trivialized by the racist phrase "all teeth and lips" (69). The second African American character, more fleshed out and more sympathetically portrayed, is the aggrieved prizefighter, the "noble-looking nigger" (77) who is chased out of Vienna by the racist white mob. This character is more substantial owing to the fact that the reader hears his story, if mediated through Bill Gorton.

Those of us who have taught Hemingway know that having students read his writing can present difficulties in the higher educational multicultural environment. Even if students haven't read anything by him, many believe that they already know Hemingway through reputation—that is, the macho personality cult he fashioned for himself—so are predisposed to brand the author a sexist. The presumption of his sexism sometimes disposes students to assume that Hemingway exhibited additional repressive ideologies, like racism. Although students rightly have been schooled to be alert for racial and other cultural stereotypes, after identifying examples of cultural labeling, students nevertheless may find it difficult to read for complex meanings. Sociological concepts like stereotype, that is, focus on the top layer of a text, and focusing on a textual act like racial labeling without considering contextual presences can inhibit deeper analyses. Chiefly due to the portrayal of the negatively depicted Jewish character Robert Cohn, though also thanks to the problematic representation of the minor black characters, an uncritical reading of *The Sun Also Rises* does little to discourage the idea that the author was anti-Semitic and a racist.

Nonetheless, the answer to this predicament does not lie in evading complex, disconcerting sex, gender, and racial issues. As a literature instructor with several decades of experience, I am convinced it would be a mistake to suggest that the racial aspects of the text are not important enough to be considered when teaching *The Sun Also Rises*. Telling students that the novel simply reflects the way many white Protestant, middle-class Americans thought about Jews and African Americans during the 1920s, moreover, is a commensurately inadequate approach. Doing so would mean avoiding the difficult racial and ethnic nature of the text, and, more importantly, such stances can't lead to a thorough exploration of the novel, as taking such a position would elide complex, key factors in the fiction's narrative. Students need to learn how to think through the way masculinity in Hemingway's text intersects with questions of race and sexuality. *The Sun Also Rises* shakes up a volatile cultural cocktail, one that still has explosive potential, and this is in fact an effective critical starting point for teaching the text.

As I discuss in the introduction to this book, Toni Morrison's early 1990s *Playing in the Dark: Whiteness and the Literary Imagination* articulates the theory of the textual "Africanist presence" (76), an absence of black being in Hemingway's and writings by other U.S. canonical literary texts that linguistically calls attention to a black phantom presence. Rather than being an exemplar of white canon making, *The Sun Also Rises*'s tangible Africanist presence presents avenues into the text that can enrich the novel's classroom reading. Brett's affirmation of her friendship with the drummer—she says he's "a great friend" (*SAR* 62) of hers—signals the blurriness of her own boundaries. Pursuing freely her own sexual desire, breaking down gender role restrictions, puts Lady Brett in a fluid situation where she may more intimately touch the world of the black drummer. Indeed, possibly the most intriguing aspect of the seemingly offhand reference to the drummer is the lingering question of whether the sex rebel Brett Ashley and the musician have had a sexual encounter. As the novel is told from Jake Barnes's point of view, such an encounter is not, in Barnes's imagination—he is obsessed with Brett's sex life—beyond the realm of possibility. Indeed, in view of Brett's uninhibited sex life, it is not an entirely implausible notion. Later in the novel, Mike Campbell rebukes her for taking up with Robert Cohn, primarily because Cohn is a Jew. Through the description of the drummer, *The Sun Also Rises* is permitted to indicate the scope of Brett's sexual revolution and disillusionment with all things conventional: class, religion, marriage, and possibly race.

Considering the passage in this way offers the occasion to talk through the complexity of point of view. Jake Barnes is a recognizably semiautobiographical version of Hemingway himself, but, as we all know, it is necessary to reiterate to students that a fictional character, no matter how similar in biographical aspects, should not be assumed to be a straightforward representation of the author. Voice of the novel's first-person singular point of view, Barnes admits to the reader that his jealousy over Brett shapes and sometimes discolors his observations. Therefore, it is *not* an act of pardoning the white author to point out that Jake, not Hemingway, is responsible for the "all teeth and lips" comment.

The depiction of the drummer, moreover, opens the door for a discussion of the expatriate African American community that existed in Paris during the Jazz Age. As Michel Fabre's *From Harlem to Paris: Black American Writers in France, 1840–1980* demonstrates, Claude McKay, Langston Hughes, Jessie Fauset, Countee Cullen, and other Harlem Renaissance, or New Negro, writers and artists resided in Paris during the 1920s, enjoying in many ways the same kind of freedom from Prohibition and related American social limitations that the Lost Generation enjoyed. New Negro writers, artists, and musicians generally found France less racist than the United States, as well. Hughes's first visit to Paris, during the 1920s, was brief, but his love of the city stayed with him for a lifetime. As black author Paule Marshall recounts in *Triangular Road*, Hughes stated, "There [Paris] you can be whatever you want to be. Totally yourself" (27).

Claude McKay knew Hemingway while living in Paris and wrote his two most famous novels in France. The first was *Home to Harlem* (1928), about an African American serviceman who deserts the U.S. military during the Great War in Europe and returns to Harlem. As I have written elsewhere, *Home to Harlem* recycles imagery from *The Sun Also Rises*; it is, on one level, a New Negro version of Hemingway's Paris-set novel, providing simultaneously homage to and critical comment on *The Sun Also Rises*. McKay's second novel, *Banjo* (1929), is set in working-class Marseilles, with its small, international community of African American, African, and Caribbean merchant sailors, rather than in chic Paris, with its cosmopolitan expatriates. As Tyler Stovall shows in *Paris Noir*, a number of black veterans also remained in or returned to France following the Great War. Like Hughes, black war vets believed that white French society was more tolerant than white American society. This led to the establishment of the "Black Montmartre" jazz scene, a kind of Parisian Harlem Renaissance second site during the Jazz Age 1920s (Stovall 62).

One assignment I have given is to have students read McKay's *Home to Harlem* after reading *The Sun Also Rises*. For upper level courses, I also assign students my own commentary, "Hemingway and McKay, Race and Nation," on the intertextual conversation between these two novels. The parallels between the novels—that is, the way in which McKay reprocesses imagery from Hemingway's texts—are palpable. *The Sun Also Rises*'s protagonist is Jake Barnes, a war veteran who is unable to consummate his love for Brett Ashley because his reproductive organ has been mutilated by the war. Barnes is a classic figure of the interwar period spiritual incapacity for regeneration. Geographical place is essential in Hemingway's novel, as Barnes lovingly depicts his adopted city of Paris in the narrative. In contrast, yet complementing Hemingway's protagonist, the principal character of *Home to Harlem* is Jake Brown, who, rather than allow himself to be scarred by the U.S. military's racism during the Great War, deserts the army and returns to his own adored *black* urban capital, Harlem. Although McKay's novel comes two years after Hemingway's, I encourage students to see that the situation is not merely one of a lesser minority author drawing on a model created by a major white writer. In fact, the two texts hold an intertextual conversation so that Hemingway's novel, with its inclusion of recognizably New Negro minor characters, could not have existed without earlier Harlem Renaissance writings by authors like McKay and works that promoted the worth of the primitive and primordial against modern social and cultural alienation.

Similarly, after students have read *The Sun Also Rises* I would suggest they read "Wedding Day" (1926), a short fiction by New Negro writer and artist Gwendolyn Bennett. Somewhat like McKay's *Home to Harlem,* the short story both complements and critiques Hemingway's text, expanding the novel's racial scope. Principally because she was not a prolific writer, Bennett is not as well known a Harlem Renaissance figure as McKay. Bennett was awarded a fellowship to study art for a year in Paris during the mid-1920s, during the period when American intellectuals, black and white, were discovering cubist, surrealist, and other avant-garde art movements of the prewar period (Patton and Honey 506). In a series of letters, she also talks about meeting Hemingway on a number of occasions and implies that she became friendly with the increasingly more celebrated fellow expat (Holcomb and Scruggs 9). After meeting Hemingway and striking up a friendship with him, Bennett tried her hand at short fiction, producing a handful of Iceberg Theory–inflected minimalist stories.

The most interesting is "Wedding Day," a black transnational short story set in Paris about a black émigré boxer, musician, and war veteran named Paul Watson. The short story is set in the Rue Pigale red-light district of Montmartre, the same eighteenth arrondissement neighborhood as Zelli's, in *The Sun Also Rises*. Like Hemingway's black prizefighter, Watson was once a successful heavyweight boxer. Unlike Hemingway's drummer, however, Watson hates whites, especially Southerners, regularly punching out white Americans who use "nigger" when referring to him, and he finally goes to prison after shooting two reactionary white American sailors. When the war breaks out, Watson is given the chance to commute his prison sentence by serving in the French military, where he is "cited many times for bravery" (Bennett 512). After the war, he returns to Black Montmartre, and, like Hemingway's deracinated black drummer, takes up jazz performance. Although he detests whites more than ever, he nevertheless takes up with a destitute young white American woman who has been forced to become a Pigale sex worker. To the amazement of his black musician friends, he falls for her and ultimately asks her to marry him, and when she ditches him, the story's enigmatic ending seems to suggest that, in a blind rage, he has murdered her. Evidently materializing from an uncontrollable motivation, clearly Freudian unconscious aggression unleashed, Paul is not consciously aware that he has committed the act of homicide against the white woman he loved.

The story's succinct style pays homage to Hemingway's unadorned, open-ended stories in *In Our Time,* most evident in Bennett's indeterminate ending. Yet the short story also offers an ironic comment on his "noble" N-word prizefighter in *The Sun Also Rises,* as the story's protagonist, Paul Watson, is a black combatant rather than a marginalized black boxer whose point of view a major white character, Bill Gorton, mediates. After they have read *The Sun Also Rises,* I have students read "Wedding Day" to encourage a discussion about the way Harlem Renaissance and Lost Generation texts hold conversations over race, sexuality, masculinity, and national identity.

More crucial than *The Sun Also Rises*'s jazz drummer is the other black character in the novel, the unnamed black prizefighter. Bill Gorton's account of the black boxer being chased out of Vienna is a portent of the arrival of fascism in central Europe. But I would add that the imagery recalls a recognizably American form of right-wing policing of minority rights, the lynch mob. Hemingway's narrative suggests that existing social modes of communication lag behind cosmopolitan consciousness, that only racist discourses are available to white Americans who, like Gorton, may sympathize with exploited and abused minority peoples.

In understanding the novel's black boxer, in particular the use of the racial epithet in describing him, it is well to keep in mind Hemingway's memorable statement in *Green Hills of Africa* that "[a]ll modern American literature comes from" Mark Twain's *The Adventures of Huckleberry Finn.* Hemingway's recognizing of Twain's text, with its compassionate portrayal of escaped slave Jim as "the best book we've had," suggests an interesting critical valence. Twain's self-sacrificing black male adult, Jim, is the literary antecedent—a noble savage—of Hemingway's noble N-word character (*GHOA* 22). In view of the fact that *Huckleberry Finn*'s runaway is repeatedly identified as "the Nigger Jim," one may see that Hemingway's noble unnamed "nigger" prizefighter is the intertextual offspring of Twain's self-denying fugitive slave. In other words, on one level Hemingway's use of the N-word, however offensive to us now, is the white author's performance of intertextuality between his novel and Twain's nation-shaping document. In this way, the young Hemingway, writing one of his earliest novels, is showing that his work carries on the imagery and discourses of, and therefore plays a part in, the history of the American literary canon. This curious detail must account for the jarring dissonance between the materialization of the racist terminology and the obvious admiration for the black boxer in *The Sun Also Rises.*

Indeed, the novel's attitude toward white American Roman Catholics displays less tolerance than the narrative's treatment of black characters. Or, at least, the way that some of the major white characters act toward Catholics is less charitable. Gorton's sympathy for those unlike himself—that is, the prizefighter—seems to be conspicuously incompatible with a later passage set on a train ride to Spain, when, angry that he is unable to have lunch because American Catholic pilgrims are being fed first, Gorton remarks to a priest: "It's enough to make a man join the Klan" (*SAR* 88). Catholics were the targets of the second-period Klan call for white Protestant purity, most of the anti-Catholic doings occurring in the urban Midwest during the 1920s.[1] Though it was bad for Catholics in the Midwest, the Klan could act with virtual impunity against African American labor and voting-rights movements in much of the South. I talk with students about the way the Klan intentionally lynched black former servicemen in their uniforms to demonstrate their commitment to proscribe African American migration from the South and attempts at fair political and legal representation.[2] A white performance of supremacy, lynching was symbolically rooted in policing black male sexuality and masculinity, thus the ritual act of emasculating corpses. It is necessary to share this history as it plays a role in reading *The Sun Also Rises*. Bill Gorton's remark reflects this posture toward Catholics, granted, in frustration and with little regard for the implications of his comments.

New Negroes, the radical black, self-articulated identity of the 1920s, were the targets of Klan and Jim Crow hegemony. Indeed, though the character is compassionately portrayed, the *noble-looking nigger* operates as a lowercasing and therefore deflating of the *New Negro* designation, the emerging black identity characterized by the Harlem Renaissance.[3] Yet this aspect of the novel is complicated by the fact that, considering the text's structural equilibrium, the black boxer is linked through imagery to two major characters, the bullfighter Pedro Romero and the pugnacious Robert Cohn. The black boxer's noble nature anticipates Romero's dignified demeanor, that is, the familiar Hemingway convention of manliness: acquitting oneself well even when adversarial forces overwhelm. Unlike Romero, the black fighter defeats his antagonist, but, in a way in contrast to Romero, he is denied recognition for the win. Romero loses his fight with Cohn but wins the war, if only fleetingly, over Brett.

Another structural correspondence as well as contrast between the black fighter and a white character is the connection with Cohn, who though capable of flattening anyone he chooses to, lacks the manly virtues. This is a troubling aspect of the text, as it raises questions about the novel's anti-Semitism, an ideology instituted around Jewish masculinity. Still, one must recognize that this anti-Jewish structure of feeling in the novel transpires, if subtly, through a positive image of a black boxer. Seen in this way, the novel's treatment of masculinity becomes complex, as it would seem that the manliest character in the narrative is the pejoratively marked, linguistically dehumanized (i.e., "nigger") black prizefighter. This situation becomes interesting because the aim of the white supremacist lynch mob is to control black masculinity, to keep in check black male sexuality. I ask my students how this imagery corresponds with the accepted wisdom that Hemingway's texts exemplify a kind of retrograde masculinist ideology. Indeed, the novel's exigent portrayal of masculinity should be understood as part of the novel's larger narrative interest in modernity, primitivism, and language performance. This is the place where, I believe, an expansive classroom conversation about *The Sun Also Rises* may begin.

Writing and Discussion Topics

1. Have students read the passages from Hemingway's *Green Hills of Africa* in which the author states that "[a]ll modern American literature comes from" Twain's *The Adventures of Huckleberry Finn*, "the best book we've had" (22), and conduct a discussion of how Hemingway's comment shapes a reading of *The Sun Also Rises*, according to the discussion above.
2. Have students read the passages on Hemingway in Morrison's *Playing in the Dark* (69–90), and hold open discussion about how her theory of the "Africanist presence" in Hemingway applies to *The Sun Also Rises*.
3. Have students read *The Sun Also Rises* followed by McKay's *Home to Harlem*, and then have them read and discuss my essay, "Hemingway and McKay, Race and Nation," on the intertextual conversation between these two novels.
4. After they have read *The Sun Also Rises*, have students read Gwendolyn Bennett's short story "Wedding Day," along with relevant passages of Fabre's *From Harlem to Paris* and Stovall's *Paris Noir*, and then have them write about the ways in which Bennett's transnational black fiction simultaneously reflects and differs from *The Sun Also Rises*.
5. Discuss masculinity in the novel and how it intersects with questions of race and ethnicity, following the discussion above. Students should consider how views of masculinity have changed since the publication of the novel in 1926.
6. Popular news media commentators and journalists have referred to American millennials as a "lost generation." Have students locate Internet

commentaries that apply this term to their own generation (or to other cohorts), and discuss, particularly with respect to how race intersects with the millennials as lost generation notion. What is the meaning of the term *lost generation?* Who determines when a particular age bracket is lost, and why it is directionless? Are ethnic minorities a part of the specific directionless generation identity?

Notes

1. See Leonard J. Moore, *Citizen Klansmen.*
2. For scholarship on black servicemen and lynching, see Vincent P. Mikkelsen, "Coming from Battle to Face a War."
3. See Alain Locke, *The New Negro.*

Teaching the Pastoral and Race in Jean Toomer, Ernest Hemingway, and Ernest Gaines

Matthew Teutsch

One portrait of Ernest J. Gaines shows the author sitting in front of a wall with three other images staring down at him. The middle picture is of his aunt Augusteen Jefferson who raised him before he left Louisiana to join his mother and stepfather in California in 1948. The other portraits are of two literary influences on Gaines: William Faulkner and Ernest Hemingway. The Yousuf Karsh photograph of Hemingway resides just above Gaines's head as Gaines looks off toward the left of the frame. The imagery is telling because Gaines has continually cited Hemingway's influence on his own writing. Speaking of Faulkner and Hemingway as influences in 1976, Gaines said, "I admire Hemingway because of this grace under pressure thing which I think is more accurate of the black man in this country than the white man" (Tooker and Hofheins 108). As well as Gaines's admiration for Hemingway's depiction of "grace under pressure," the stylistic elements of Hemingway also appear in his work. One needs to only look at the first few pages of Gaines's first novel, *Catherine Carmier* (1964), to see this influence.

Even though Gaines discusses authors such as Hemingway, Faulkner, Steinbeck, Tolstoy, Joyce, Turgenev, and others as influences, he says that African American authors did not influence him when he began to write and to formulate his voice. Of course, this could be for various reasons, one being that Gaines would not have found authors like Claude McKay, Richard Wright, Zora Neal Hurston, and others upon first entering a California library in 1948. However, even though he did not find these authors in the library when he first crossed the library's threshold, they did circuitously influence his burgeoning writing style, most notably, Jean Toomer's *Cane* (1923). Gaines has stated that if he had read *Cane* before he developed his own voice, the genre-breaking text would have served as influence; however, when he finally read it in the 1960s, his voice was already, according to Gaines, established.

In an unpublished interview by Reese N. Epstein in 1974, Gaines comments briefly on Toomer while speaking about the history of African American literature. After mentioning slave narratives, he says, "Then you had the black Harlem [R]enaissance-type work which was different from slave narratives in that they're looking for much more than the hardship of our people. They're looking for another kind of beauty of our people; the joys as well as the sorrows and problems of our people. I'm thinking about books like Cain [sic], especially Cain [sic], by Gene Touma [sic]." Key here is that Gaines points out that Toomer writes about "the joys as well as the sorrows" (Epstein 5) of African Americans because Gaines does a similar thing with his work. Later, in 1978, Gaines told the *Southwestern Review*,

> I think that there's nothing in Black literature to compare to [*Cane*]—that man is more original than any other Black writer. He is as original as any American writer. He was doing in *Cane* what—I'm sure Hemingway read *Cane*. You see *Cane* came out early, around '23, and Hemingway didn't start publishing his stuff till around '26–'27.[1] What Toomer was doing, those chapters, and those little poetic things between the chapters, Hemingway does the same thing with the *In Our Time* stories—First he writes a story then these little small passages. (Rickels 134)

Gaines saw the similarities between Toomer and Hemingway in style and form, even stating, Toomer "is an influence" on Hemingway, "I'm pretty sure of it" (Rickels 134). With this in mind, it can only be acknowledged that Toomer did have an indirect influence on Gaines.

This essay addresses the connections between Toomer, Hemingway, and Gaines by examining each author's use of the pastoral in their works. I will show how each author's deployment of the bucolic setting informs our understanding of them as modernist authors and brings to light their interconnectedness. Each can be considered a modernist author because each deals with, as Margaret E. Wright-Cleveland says when discussing Toomer and Hemingway, three essential modernist tenants: "the relationship of the past to the present; the relationship between the individual and the land or nature; and the role of language in defining identity" (152). These aspects of modernism can be seen in Toomer's "Avey," Hemingway's "Big Two-Hearted River," and Gaines's

"The Sky Is Gray."[2] By examining these three texts together, I will show how and why they should be taught in conjunction, especially when it comes to studying Hemingway and race.

The main way to discuss Toomer, Hemingway, and Gaines together is by looking at how each author uses the *pastoral* to either escape or come to grips with the present. The pastoral, simply put, incorporates a green space away from the modernization and mechanization of the present, a place where one can find solace away from the encroachment of modernity. For Hemingway, this appears in the landscape that Nick Adams retreats to after coming home from World War I. For Toomer and Gaines, the pastoral is not a solitary place but one of community that their characters leave and recall when faced with modernity. Leo Marx's seminal work *The Machine in the Garden* examines the pastoral in American literature, and when discussing the "complex pastoral," Marx states that Hemingway exemplifies it through his acknowledgement of history:

> The work of Faulkner, Frost, Hemingway, and West comes to mind. Again and again they invoke the image of a green landscape—a terrain either wild or, if cultivated, rural—as a symbolic repository of meaning and value. But at the same time, they acknowledge the power of a counterforce, a machine or some other symbol of the forces which have stripped the old ideal of most, if not all, of its meaning. Complex pastoralism, to put it another way, acknowledges the *reality of history*. (362–63; emphasis added)

Donald M. Shaffer Jr. says that while complex pastoralism looks toward an idyllic, pastoral space of enlightenment, "it simultaneously acknowledges the intractably built structures of modern society" (113). This aspect can be seen in Hemingway's "Big Two-Hearted River" when Nick Adams walks through the scorched remains of Seney and enters the "green landscape" (Marx 362) that still carries remnants of Seney's charred earth through the presence of the grasshoppers and burnt tree stumps. Like Hemingway, Toomer and Gaines also employ this idea of complex pastoralism, a way of looking to the past, as Toomer does with the South and Gaines does with community, to expound upon "the reality of history." Throughout the second section of *Cane*, the protagonists look back to the South for strength and identity. In Gaines's "The Sky Is Gray," James and Octavia leave the community and enter the urban environment of Bayonne.

While each author shows signs of complex pastoralism, Toomer's and Gaines's use of the pastoral incorporate another aspect. Speaking of the pastoral in *Cane,* Lucinda H. MacKethan states that Toomer "mold[ed] his book into a version of the southern pastoral perceived with the black man's double vision of deep belonging and forced alienation" because of his concern over the African American's place in the modern world (426). "Avey," from Toomer's *Cane,* shows this through the narrator's continual recalling of the South, specifically during the scene at Soldier's Home. Gaines's "The Sky Is Gray" shows this "double vision" in James's relationship with his family and community in the quarters and in his exposure to the harsh realities of racism and oppression in Bayonne. Nick Adams in Hemingway's story does not necessarily show this double vision because upon entering the sanctuary of the valley his alienation disappears and he becomes overwhelmed with happiness, even if he notices the charred grasshoppers.

In "Avey," Toomer brings together the rural and the urban in a similar manner as Gaines's "The Sky Is Gray." The protagonist of "Avey" looks to garner affection from Avey; however, she appears to not necessarily care about the young man's advances. He envies the college student who Avey visits on the top floor of the apartment building and who her mother pushes her to marry. Shaffer argues that the distance within the relationship between Avey and the narrator "is analogous to the disjuncture between the urban life of the North and the rural, pastoral experience of the South" (122). This "disjuncture" can be seen in the final scene of the story when Avey and the protagonist sit together in the city park overlooking Washington, D.C. While sitting with Avey in the park, the narrator muses that he always goes to Soldier's Home when he wants to see "the simple beauty of another's soul" (45). The green space in the middle of the urban city provides him with the opportunity to look for truth, in the pastoral, and to reminisce about his past in the South. As "Washington lies below," he begins to ruminate on the wind and its direction: "And when the wind is from the South, soil of my homeland falls like a fertile shower upon the lean streets of the city" (46). His movement, from the rural South to the urban North, appears in this quote as the South's soil falls upon the North's streets in the same manner that saw southern African Americans moving from the rural South to the industrial North during the Great Migration. Recalling the South again, the protagonist hears a band in the distance playing a march and wants them to stop, preferring to hear the Howard Glee Club singing "Deep River, Deep River" instead of the marching band whose "playing was like a tin spoon in one's mouth" (46).

Throughout the story, the confrontation between the rural and the urban appears. At the very beginning, as the narrator and his friends wait for Avey to return from visiting the college fellow, they all sit on the curb and begin to hack at the trees on the street: "I like to think now that there was a *hidden purpose* in the way we hacked them with our knives. I like to feel like *something deep in me responded to the trees,* the young trees that whinnied like colts impatient to be let free" (42; emphasis added). Underneath the "arch lights" that illuminate the sprawling city streets, the protagonist feels a pull toward the natural trees and responds to it. This response repeats at the end of the story when the speaker says he wants to wake Avey and "get up and whittle at the boxes of young trees" (46). The tension between the southern pastoral and the northern urban does not become resolved in the story, either through Avey or the narrator. Telling Avey about his past and his development, the protagonist notes the incapability of Washington to understand the needs of both himself and Avey as they try to navigate the new urban environment while recalling and drawing upon their past. Ultimately, this cannot be accomplished and the park becomes, as Shaffer notes, "a liminal point in the narrative where both ideals come into contact, the conflict of rural and urban meanings remains unresolved" (123). The story ends abruptly with the narrator wanting to wake Avey and then simply calling her "Orphan-woman," a person stuck between the past and the present, not able to return to the pastoral or to move forward to the urban.

Hemingway's use of the pastoral in "Big Two-Hearted River" differs from Toomer's because Nick finds happiness in his situation. The story portrays Nick returning from war to find solace and solitude in a tranquil, pastoral setting in northern Michigan. Whereas the anonymous narrator and Avey in Toomer's story fail to achieve a complete peace in the park, Nick finds peace and comfort in his pastoral setting, one that takes him away from the encroachment of modernity. After passing the burned remains of Seney, Nick ventures toward the river while carrying the "heavy" pack on his back. When he sets up camp for the night and erects his tent, Nick crawls in and becomes happy because "[i]t smelled pleasantly of canvas. Already there was something mysterious and homelike. Nick was happy" (139). Inside the tent, and in the country, "[n]othing could touch him" because "he was in his home where he had made it" (139). The landscape does not provide any obstacles to Nick. He finds sustenance in the fish from the river that he catches with untainted grasshoppers, and he does not encounter any foreboding individuals or animals in his journey as James does in Gaines's "The Sky Is Gray." The swamp remains safely farther down the river as a place "[h]e did not feel like going," and unlike his encounter with Bugs and Ad in "The Battler," no other human interferes with his "happy" retreat (155). Nick's movement away from Seney and farther into the wilderness works as a way of reformulating the past. Frederic J. Svoboda shows that Nick could not have "walked in a grove of old growth pines" outside of Seney due to the extensive logging of the area, and that through the incorporation of a forested area "Nick seems to journey back in time to the forest primeval" (39) While all of this makes it look like Nick travels into an ancient, pastoral landscape, hints of others encroaching or attempting to encroach on the landscape appear.

Hemingway's story contains undertones of a Native American presence as Philip Melling argues and more importantly an African American presence in the form of the charred grasshoppers that Nick encounters. Sitting next to a charred stump, Nick begins to smoke and observe the grasshoppers around him:

> The grasshopper was *black*. As he had walked along the road, climbing, he had started many grasshoppers from the dust. They were all *black*. They were not the big grasshoppers with yellow and *black* or red and *black* wings whirring out from their *black* wing sheathing as they fly up. These were just ordinary hoppers, but all a sooty *black* in color. Nick had wondered about them as he walked, without really thinking about them. Now, as he watched the *black* hopper that was nibbling at the wool of his sock with his fourway lip, he realized that they had all turned *black* from living in the burned-over land. He realized that the fire must have come the year before, but the grasshoppers were all *black* now. He wondered how long they would stay that way. (135–36; emphasis added)

Hemingway uses the word *black* nine times in the paragraph above. Ian Marshall argues that even though there is little discussion of Hemingway's political activity regarding the summer of 1919, Hemingway would have paid close attention to the race and labor relations of the time. In 1919 Hemingway made his trip to Seney with Al Walker and Jack Pentecost after World War I. That year also marks one of the worst summers for race relations, earning it the name "The Red Summer." Elaborating on this connection, Marshall says, "Like the blackened hopper that nibbles at Nick's sock, the plight of blacks and the working class generally is noticed but ignored in Hemingway's literary and creative imagination" (208). Nick notices the blackened grasshoppers; however, choosing grasshoppers to use as bait, he selects "about fifty of the medium browns," not the black, soot-covered ones (145). Interestingly, the paragraph where Nick gathers grasshoppers and places them in the bottle does not contain the word "black"; instead, the only adjectives used to describe the grasshoppers are "good" and "medium-sized brown" (145). What does this mean? Even though Nick takes notice of the black grasshopper nibbling at his foot, he decides to choose the "normal" grasshoppers for his bait, ignoring the darkened ones. The black ones appear on the edge of the burnt town then disappear as Nick makes his way deeper into his restful landscape. Ultimately, these grasshoppers do not have a place within Nick's bucolic world.

While the pastoral Michigan countryside in Hemingway's story can be seen as a place of solace and refuge for Nick after the war, the rural landscapes of Gaines's southern Louisiana take on a different image. Here, the pastoral becomes more in line with Toomer's "double vision" mentioned earlier. Like Toomer, Gaines cannot escape the past of slavery and racism that haunts the southern landscape, and because of this, "Gaines does not romanticize rural life in his [works];" instead, he points out how the harsh working conditions and lingering effects of slavery "can drain both body and spirit" (Shelton 24). Gaines's "The Sky Is Gray" displays these draining aspects of the southern pastoral through his descriptions of rural life brushing up against the modernity found in Bayonne. Upon entering Bayonne, James notes that he sees "grass shooting right out of the sidewalk" (93). The urban and the rural meet in this central image. Unlike the space provided for Avey and the protagonist in Toomer's story, the image of grass poking through the sidewalk shows the harsh realities that James will face on his trip into town.

Early in the story, eight-year-old James recalls how his idyllic, rural existence gets uprooted when his mother, Octavia, calls on him to kill two birds that he and Ty caught. The young boys wished to play with the birds; however, Octavia forces James to kill them so the family will have food to eat. Reflecting on the experience, James describes how killing the birds made him think about being a man: "They was so little, though. They was so little. I 'member how I picked the feathers off them and cleaned them and helt them over the fire. Then we all ate them. Ain't had but a little bitty piece each, but we all had a little bitty piece and everybody just looked at me 'cause they was so proud" (90).

James continues by ruminating about what would happen to him and Ty if his mother went away like his father did. Ultimately, the idea of being innocent and playing with the birds that the young siblings trapped goes by the wayside. Octavia teaches her son the harsh realities of an oppressive society that causes them to have to scrounge for food, each getting "a little bitty piece" of the birds. In the rural setting, racism does not make an overt appearance. Instead, Gaines focuses on James and his family as they struggle to survive. In many ways, this technique, like the examples of racism in Bayonne presented below, recalls Hemingway's use of understatement that he deploys with the grasshoppers.

Before heading to Bayonne, James talks about the quarters where he and his family reside. This space can be seen as an oppressive area that limits the movement of its residents. As Charles Rowell puts it, they "are enclosed communities whose limited space forces each inhabitant into the private life of others" (739). The confined space causes the occupants to work together to survive, bringing their private lives into the public arena. James's killing of the birds for dinner shows this because he does not just kill the animals for his brother, mother, and himself. He kills the birds for Auntie and Monsieur Bayonne and others who remain nameless. "Everybody" looked at him after he killed the feathery creatures and they all expressed pride in his actions. This community disappears as James and Octavia head for Bayonne, where the rural and the urban collide. Once James leaves the quarters, he is alone with his mother to face the overt racism of Bayonne.

Upon heading for Bayonne, James becomes removed from the community aspects of the quarters, which manifest themselves in the early part of the story. Just as Hemingway acknowledges and then dismisses the presence of African Americans in his story with the "black" grasshoppers, Gaines incorporates understatement to show that James has left the confines of his community for the harsh realities of prejudice and racism when he comes in contact with the white world in Bayonne. Gaines does not overtly have James and Octavia encounter racism through contact with hostile whites or Cajuns. Instead, Gaines subtly points out that racial discrimination exists. When the bus appears, mother and son get on, and James says, "When I pass the little sign that say 'White' and 'Colored,' I start looking for a seat" (91). On the entire bus ride, this is all that James mentions regarding segregation. Walking through town, James notices white children playing outside at a school and people eating in a café; Octavia keeps him moving forward, telling him to "keep [his] eyes in front" (93). Passing the courthouse, James sees a flag blowing the air. He comments, "This flag ain't like the one we got at school. The one here ain't got but a handful of stars. One at school got a big pile of stars—one for every state" (93). James, as an eight-year-old boy, does not say that the flag flying over the courthouse is the Confederate flag. All of these instances are fleeting, taking up no more than a sentence here or there. Reading the story, one may look over these subtle references to prejudice and segregation in Bayonne just as one might run past Hemingway's seemingly innocuous descriptions of "black" grasshoppers. However, they should not be ignored. Unlike Hemingway, Gaines confronts the problems with an oppressive society, specifically by having the student in the dentist's office question America's supposed equality when refuting an African American patient who claims she is a citizen: "Citizens have certain rights.... Name me one right that you have. One right, granted by the Constitution, that you can exercise in Bayonne" (101).

Ultimately, the three authors discussed in this essay either confront race or leave it as an underlying theme in the stories examined. While one could teach other works by these authors concurrently, teaching these stories allows for a look not only into race and the way that the authors explore it but also at their use of the pastoral to comment on white and African American responses to the urban environment. While Hemingway eschews Nick coming in contact with modernity, except in the form of Seney's burnt remains, Toomer and Gaines have their characters come face to face with the urban environment and what it means to them as African Americans. Nick does not have to worry about this because he can find his space and be "happy," even with the trauma of war. The protagonist of Toomer's story, Avey, James, and Octavia do not have this luxury because of their race. They must confront "the reality of history" that subjects them to racism and oppression.

Notes

1. Hemingway's first collection, *Three Stories and Ten Poems*, appeared in 1923 while *In Our Time* debuted in 1925.

2. While Hemingway's story has two parts, I will be discussing both of them. I will just use "Big Two-Hearted River" as the title.

Works Cited

Atkinson, Michael. *Hemingway Deadlights.* New York: St. Martin's, 2009.
Bakara, Amiri. *The LeRoi Jones/Amiri Baraka Reader.* Ed. William J. Harris. New York: Thunder's Mouth Press, 2000. 217.
Baker, Carlos. *Ernest Hemingway: A Life Story.* New York: Scribner, 1969.
———. *Hemingway: The Writer as Artist.* 4th ed. Princeton, NJ: Princeton UP, 1980.
Baker, Houston A. *Modernism and the Harlem Renaissance.* Chicago: U of Chicago P, 1987.
Balderrama, Francisco, and Raymond Rodríguez. *Decade of Betrayal: Mexican Repatriation in the 1930s.* Albuquerque: U of New Mexico P, 2016.
Banks, James A. "Transforming the Mainstream Curriculum." *Phi Delta Kappan* 75:1 (1993): 22–28.
Barnard, Rita. "Modern American Fiction." *The Cambridge Companion to American Modernism.* Ed. Walter Kalaidjian. New York: Cambridge UP, 2005. 39–67.
Barr, R. B., and J. Tagg. "From Teaching to Learning: A New Paradigm for Undergraduate Education." *Change* 27 (1995): 12–25.
Bateson, Daniel, et al. "Immorality from Empathy-Induced Altruism." *Journal of Personality and Social Psychology* 68 (1995): 1042–54.
Bauer, Margaret D. "Forget the Legend and Read the Work: Teaching Two Stories by Ernest Hemingway." *College Literature* 30.3 (2003): 124–37.
Bennett, Gwendolyn. "Wedding Day." *Double-Take: A Revisionist Harlem Renaissance Anthology.* Ed. Venetria Patton and Maureen Honey. New Brunswick, NJ: Rutgers UP, 2001. 511–16.
Benson, Jackson J. "Patterns of Connection and Their Development in Hemingway's *In Our Time.*" In Reynolds, *Critical.* 103–20.
Biggs, John. "Enhancing Teaching through Constructive Alignment." *Higher Education* 32 (1996): 347–64.
———. "The Role of Metalearning in Study Processes." *British Journal of Educational Psychology* 55 (1985): 185–212.
———. *Student Approaches to Learning and Studying.* Hawthorn: Australian Council for Educational Research, 1987.
———. "What Do Inventories of Students' Learning Processes Really Measure? A Theoretical Review and Clarification." *British Journal of Educational Psychology* 63 (1993): 3–19.

Biggs, J., and K. F. Collis. *Evaluating the Quality of Learning: The SOLO Taxonomy (Structure of the Observed Learning Outcome)*. New York: Academic Press, 1982.

Biggs, J., and Tang, C. *Teaching for Quality Learning at University*. Berkshire: Society for Research into Higher Education & Open University Press, 2007.

Blackbird, Andrew J. *History of the Ottawa and Chippewa Indians of Michigan; A Grammar of Their Language, and Personal and Family History of the Author*. Ypsilanti, MI: Ypsilantian Job Printing House, 1887.

Bracher, Mark. *Radical Pedagogy*. New York: Palgrave, 2006.

Bransford, J. D., A. L. Brown, and R. R. Cocking, eds. *How People Learn*. Washington, D.C.: National Academy Press, 2000.

Brookfield, S. D. *Becoming a Critically Reflective Teacher*. San Francisco: Jossey-Bass, 1995.

Bruccoli, Matthew J., ed. *The Only Thing That Counts: The Ernest Hemingway-Maxwell Perkins Correspondence*. Columbia: U of South Carolina P, 1996.

Burbules, Nicholas C., and Rupert Berk. "Critical Thinking and Critical Pedagogy: Relations, Differences, and Limits." *Critical Theories in Education*. Ed. Thomas S. Popkewitz and Lynn Fendler. New York: Routledge, 1999. 45–66.

Burhans, Clinton S. "The Complex Unity of *In Our Time*." In Reynolds, *Critical*. 88–103.

Burkhart, Dan. "Hemingway Books Sold Have Billings Connection." *Billings Gazette*, 14 Dec. 2011. Web. <http://billingsgazette.com/news/local/hemingway-books-sold-have-billings-connection/article_7968fb97-706d-54c9-9682-8c321f01337e.html>.

Capellán, Angel. *Hemingway and the Hispanic World*. Ann Arbor, MI: UMI Research Press, 1977.

Castro, Rafaela. *Chicano Folklore: A Guide to the Folktales, Traditions, Rituals, and Religious Practices of Mexican-Americans*. New York: Oxford UP, 2000.

Chickering, A. W., and Z. F. Gamson. "Seven Principles for Good Practice in Undergraduate Education." *AAHE Bulletin* (Mar. 1987): 3–7.

Cooper, Stephen. "Race and Artistic Freedom in Langston Hughes' 'Home.'" *Short Story* 10.1 (2002): 89–96.

Cowley, Malcolm. *Exile's Return: A Literary Odyssey of the 1920s*. New York: Viking Press, 1951.

Curnutt, Kirk. *Ernest Hemingway and the Expatriate Modernist Movement*. Detroit: Gale Group, 2000.

Damon, William. *The Moral Child*. New York: Free Press, 1988.

Darder, Antonia. "What Is Critical Pedagogy?" *Key Questions for Educators*. Ed. William Hare and John P. Portelli. Halifax, NS: Edphil Books, 2005. 113–17.

Donaldson, Scott, ed. *The Cambridge Companion to Ernest Hemingway*. New York: Cambridge UP, 1996.

DeFalco, Joseph. *The Hero in Hemingway's Short Stories*. Pittsburgh: U of Pittsburgh P, 1963.

de Jongh, James. *Vicious Modernism: Black Harlem and the Literary Imagination*. New York: Cambridge UP, 1990.

Dewey, John. *Experience and Education*. New York: Simon and Schuster, 1938.

———. *How We Think*. 2nd ed. London: Dover, 1933.

Donovan, S., and J. D. Bransford. *How Students Learn: History, Mathematics, and Science in the Classroom*. Washington, D.C.: National Academies Press, 2005.

Douglas, Aaron. "Rebirth." In Locke. 56.

Douglas, Ann. *Terrible Honesty: Mongrel Manhattan in the 1920s.* New York: Farrar, Straus and Giroux, 1995.

Dudley, Marc. *Hemingway, Race, and Art: Bloodlines and the Color Line.* Kent, OH: Kent State UP, 2012.

Eby, Carl P. *Hemingway's Fetishism: Psychoanalysis and the Mirror of Manhood.* Albany: SUNY Press, 1999.

Ekman, Paul, ed. *Darwin and Facial Expression: A Century of Research in Review.* New York: Academic Press, 1973.

Entwistle, N. J. *Styles of Learning and Teaching: An Integrated Outline of Educational Psychology for Students, Teachers and Lecturers.* Chichester, UK: John Wiley, 1981.

Epstein, Reese N. "Interview with Ernest J. Gaines." Box 19, Folder 14. Ernest J. Gaines Collection. Ernest J. Gaines Center, University of Louisiana at Lafayette. Unprocessed.

Fabre, Michel. *From Harlem to Paris: Black American Writers in France, 1840–1980.* Urbana: U of Illinois P, 1993.

Fairclough, Norman. *Language and Power.* New York: Longman, 1989.

Fetterley, Judith. *The Resisting Reader: A Feminist Approach to American Fiction.* Bloomington: Indiana UP, 1977.

"Fight to Preserve Land to Papooses Who Are the Prey of 'Land Grafters.'" *Petoskey Evening News and Daily Resorter,* 14 Oct. 1915.

Fisher, Rudolph. "The City of Refuge." In Locke. 57–74.

Freire, Paulo. *Pedagogy of the Oppressed.* Translated by M. B. Ramos. New York: Continuum International Publishing Group, 2000.

Gaines, Ernest J. "The Sky Is Gray." *Bloodline.* New York: Norton, 1976. 83–117.

Graff, Gerald. *Beyond the Culture Wars: How Teaching the Conflicts Can Revitalize American Education.* New York: Norton, 1992.

Gross, Ariela J. "'The Caucasian Cloak': Mexican Americans and the Politics of Whiteness in the Twentieth-Century Southwest." *Critical Race Theory: The Cutting Edge.* Philadelphia: Temple UP, 2013.

Gruber Godfrey, Laura. "Hemingway and Cultural Geography: The Landscape of Logging in 'The End of Something.'" *Hemingway: Eight Decades of Criticism.* Ed. Linda Wagner-Martin. East Lansing: Michigan State UP, 2009.

Hattie, J. A. C., and G. T. L. Brown. *Cognitive Processes in asTTle: The SOLO Taxonomy.* Auckland: University of Auckland/Ministry of Education, 2004.

Haviland, Jeannette, and Mary Lelwica. "The Induced Affect Response: 10-Week-Old Infant's Responses to Three Emotion Expressions." *Developmental Psychology* 23 (1987): 97–104.

Hemingway, Ernest. "The Battler." In *Complete Short Stories.* 95–104.

———. *The Complete Short Stories of Ernest Hemingway: The Finca Vigía Edition.* New York: Scribner, 1987.

———. *Death in the Afternoon.* New York: Scribner, 1932.

———. *Ernest Hemingway: Selected Letters 1917–1961.* Ed. Carlos Baker. New York: Scribner, 2003.

———. *A Farewell to Arms.* New York: Scribner, 1995.

———. *Green Hills of Africa.* New York: Scribner, 1935.

———. *In Our Time.* New York: Boni and Liveright, 1925.
———. *A Moveable Feast: The Restored Edition.* New York: Scribner, 2010.
———. *The Nick Adams Stories.* New York: Scribner, 1972.
———. "Soldier's Home." 1925. In *Complete Short Stories.* 111–16.
———. *The Sun Also Rises.* New York: Scribner, 1926.
———. *To Have and Have Not.* New York: Scribner, 1984.
Historic Bay View Cottages: Bay View, Michigan, 1875–1975. Bay View, MI: Bay View Library Board, 1975.
Hoff, Hild E. "'Self' and 'Other' in Meaningful Interaction: Using Fiction to Develop Intercultural Competence in the English Classroom." *Tidsskriftet FoU i praksis* 7.2 (2013): 27–50.
Hoffman, Frederick J. *The Twenties: American Writing in the Postwar Decade.* 1955. New York: Free Press, 1965.
Holcomb, Gary Edward. "Hemingway and McKay, Race and Nation." In Holcomb and Scruggs. 133–50.
Holcomb, Gary Edward, and Charles Scruggs, eds. *Hemingway and the Black Renaissance.* Columbus: Ohio State UP, 2012.
———. "Introduction." In Holcomb and Scruggs. 1–26.
Hughes, Langston. *The Collected Works of Langston Hughes, Volume 15: The Short Stories.* Ed. R. Baxter Miller. Columbia: U of Missouri P, 2002.
———. "Home." 1934. In *Collected Works.* 37–45.
———. "I, Too." In Locke. 145.
———. *I Wonder as I Wander: An Autobiographical Journey.* 1956. New York: Hill and Wang, 1993.
———. "Minstrel Man." In Locke. 144.
James, R., C. McInnis, and M. Devlin. *Assessing Learning in Australian Universities.* Melbourne: Centre for the Study of Higher Education, 2012.
Johnston, Kenneth G. "'The Butterfly and the Tank': Casualties of War." *Studies in Short Fiction* 26.2 (1989): 183–86.
Joughin, G. "Assessment, Learning and Judgement in Higher Education: A Critical Review." *Assessment, Learning and Judgement in Higher Education.* Ed. G. Joughin. New York: Springer, 2009. 13–28.
———. "Introduction: Referencing Assessment." In *Assessment, Learning and Judgement.* 1–12.
Justice, Hilary. *The Bones of the Others.* Kent, OH: Kent State UP, 2006.
Kinnamon, Kenneth. "Hemingway and Politics." *The Cambridge Companion to Ernest Hemingway.* Ed. Scott Donaldson. New York: Cambridge UP, 1996. 149–69.
Kirschke, Amy Helene. *Aaron Douglas: Art, Race and the Harlem Renaissance.* Jackson: U of Mississippi P, 1995.
Kramsch, Claire. *Context and Culture in Language Teaching.* Oxford: Oxford UP, 1993.
Krathwohl, David R. "A Revision of Bloom's Taxonomy: An Overview." *Theory into Practice* 41.4 (2002): 212–18.
Larsen, Steen F., and Seilman, Uffe. "Personal Meanings while Reading Literature." *Text* 8 (1988): 411–29.

Leigh, David J. "*In Our Time:* The Interchapters as Structural Guide to Psychological Pattern." In Reynolds, *Critical*. 130–38.

Levinas, Emmanuel. *Ethics and Infinity: Conversations with Philippe Nemo.* Translated by Richard A. Cohen. Pittsburgh: Duquesne UP, 1985.

Lewis, David Levering. *When Harlem Was in Vogue.* New York: Knopf, 1981.

Locke, Alain, ed. "Foreword." In Locke. 3–16.

———. "Negro Youth Speaks." In Locke. 47–53.

———. *The New Negro.* 1925. New York: Macmillan, 1992.

———. "The New Negro." In Locke. 3–16.

Lowe, John, ed. *Conversations with Ernest Gaines.* Jackson: UP of Mississippi, 1995.

Lynn, Kenneth S. "Hemingway's Private War." *Commentary* 72 (July 1981): 24–33.

MacKethan, Lucinda H. "Jean Toomer's *Cane:* A Pastoral Problem." *Mississippi Quarterly* 28.4 (1975): 423–34.

Maier, Kevin. "Hunting." *Ernest Hemingway in Context.* Ed. Debra A. Moddelmog and Suzanne del Gizzo. Cambridge: Cambridge UP, 2013. 267–76.

Marshall, Ian. "Rereading Hemingway: Rhetorics of Whiteness, Labor, and Identity." In Holcomb and Scruggs. 117–213.

Marshall, Paule. *Triangular Road: A Memoir.* New York: Basic Civitas Books, 2009.

Martínez, George A. "Mexican Americans and Whiteness." *Critical Race Theory: The Cutting Edge.* Philadelphia: Temple UP, 2013.

Marton, F., D. Hounsell, and N. Entwistle. *The Experience of Learning: Implications for Teaching and Studying in Higher Education.* 2nd ed. Edinburgh: Scottish Academic Press, 1997.

Marton, F., and R. Saljo. "On Qualitative Differences in Learning—1: Outcome and Process." *British Journal of Educational Psychology* 46 (1976): 4–11.

Marx, Leo. *The Machine in the Garden: Technology and the Pastoral Ideal in America.* New York: Oxford UP, 1964.

Mayer, Richard E. "Rote Versus Meaningful Learning." *Theory into Practice* 41.4 (2002): 226–32.

McKay, Claude. "White Houses." In Locke. 134.

Melling, Philip. "'There Were Many Indians in the Story': Hidden History in Hemingway's 'Big Two-Hearted River.'" *Hemingway Review* 28.2 (2009): 45–65.

Mellow, James R. *Hemingway: A Life without Consequences.* Boston: Houghton Mifflin, 1992.

Meltzoff, Andrew. "Infant Imitation After a 1-Week Delay." *Developmental Psychology* 24 (1988): 470–76.

Mikkelsen, Vincent P. "Coming from Battle to Face a War: The Lynching of Black Soldiers in the World War I Era." Electronic Theses, Treatises and Dissertations, Paper 2443, 2007.

Moddelmog, Debra A., and Suzanne del Gizzo, eds. *Ernest Hemingway in Context.* Cambridge: Cambridge UP, 2013.

Moore, Leonard J. *Citizen Klansmen: The Ku Klux Klan in Indiana, 1921–1928.* Chapel Hill: U of North Carolina P, 1991.

Morrison, Toni. *Playing in the Dark: Whiteness and the Literary Imagination.* Cambridge, MA: Harvard UP, 1992.

———. "Unspeakable Things Unspoken: The Afro-American Experience in American Literature." *Michigan Quarterly Review* 28.1 (1989): 1–34.
Oak Leaves. 22 Aug. 1902. 8.
———. 4 Mar. 1904.
———. 29 Apr. 1914.
———. 2 May 1914. 3.
Oatley, Keith. "Why Fiction Might be Twice as True as Fact." *Review of General Psychology* 3.2 (1999): 101–17.
Ostrom, Hans. *Langston Hughes: A Study of the Short Fiction*. New York: Twayne, 1993.
Ott, Mark P. "A Shared Language of American Modernism: Hemingway and the Harlem Renaissance." In Holcomb and Scruggs. 27–37.
Patton, Venetria, and Maureen Honey, eds. "Gwendolyn Bennett." *Double-Take: A Revisionist Harlem Renaissance Anthology*. New Brunswick, NJ: Rutgers UP, 2001. 506.
Pflüg, Melissa A. *Ritual and Myth in Odawa Revitalization: Reclaiming a Sovereign Place*. Norman: U of Oklahoma P, 1998.
Plath, James. "On a Fairy's Wing: Hints of Fitzgerald in Hemingway's 'The Butterfly and the Tank.'" *Journal of the Short Story in English* 43 (2004): 75–85.
Porter, James A. "The New Negro and Modern Art." *The New Negro Thirty Years Afterward*. Washington, D.C.: Howard UP, 1955.
Prosser, M., and K. Trigwell. *Understanding Learning and Teaching, on Deep and Surface Learning*. Philadelphia: Society for Research into Higher Education & Open University Press, 1999.
Putnam, Robert. *Bowling Alone: The Collapse and the Revival of American Community*. New York: Simon and Schuster, 2000.
Rampersad, Arnold. "Introduction." In Locke. ix–xxvii.
Ramsden, P. *Learning to Teach in Higher Education*. London: Routledge, 1992.
Reissland, Nadja. "Neonatal Imitation in the First Hour of Life: Observations in Rural Nepal." *Developmental Psychology* 24 (1988): 464–69.
Reynolds, Michael S., ed. *Critical Essays on Ernest Hemingway's* In Our Time. Boston: G. K. Hall, 1983.
———. *Hemingway: The 1930s*. New York: Norton, 1997.
———. *Hemingway's Reading, 1910–1940: An Inventory*. Princeton, NJ: Princeton UP, 1981.
———. *The Young Hemingway*. New York: Blackwell, 1986.
Rickels, Patricia. "An Interview with Ernest Gaines." *Conversations with Ernest Gaines*. Ed. John Lowe. Jackson: U of Mississippi P, 1995. 119–36.
Rieser, Andrew C. *The Chautauqua Moment: Protestants, Progressives, and the Culture of Modern Liberalism*. New York: Columbia UP, 2003.
Riley, Charles A. *The Jazz Age in France*. New York: Henry N. Abrams, 2004.
Rowell, Charles. "The Quarters: Ernest Gaines and the Sense of Place." *Southern Review* 21.3 (1985): 733–50.
Sanders, Mark A. "American Modernism and the New Negro Renaissance." *The Cambridge Companion to American Modernism*. Ed. Walter Kalaidjian. New York: Cambridge UP, 2005.

Schmalzbauer, Leah. "Gender on a New Frontier: Mexican Migration in the Rural Mountain West." *Gender and Society* 23.6 (2009): 747–67.
Shaffer, Donald M., Jr. "'When the Sun Goes Down': The Ghetto Pastoral Mode in Jean Toomer's *Cane*." *Southern Literary Journal* 45.1 (2012): 111–28.
Shelton, Frank W. "Of Machines and Men: Pastoralism in Gaines's Fiction." *Critical Reflections on the Fiction of Ernest J. Gaines*. Ed. David C. Estes. Athens: U of Georgia P, 1994. 12–29.
Singer, Peter. *The Expanding Circle: Ethics, Evolution, and Moral Progress*. Princeton, NJ: Princeton UP, 2011.
Stephens, Robert O. *Hemingway's Nonfiction: The Public Voice*. Chapel Hill, NC: U of North Carolina P, 1968.
Stewart, Matthew. *Modernism and Tradition in Ernest Hemingway's* In Our Time. New York: Camden House, 2001.
Stovall, Tyler. *Paris Noir: African Americans in the City of Light*. Boston: Houghton Mifflin, 1996.
Strong, Amy L. *Race and Identity in Hemingway's Fiction*. New York: Palgrave Macmillan, 2008.
Strychacz, Thomas. *Hemingway's Theaters of Masculinity*. Baton Rouge: Louisiana State UP, 2003.
Summers, Martin. *Nationalism, Race Consciousness, and the Constructions of Black Middle Class Masculinity During the New Negro Era, 1915–1930*. Dissertation, Rutgers University, 1997. UMI 1997.
Svinicki, M. D. "IDEA Paper #41: Student Goal-Orientation, Motivation, and Learning." POD-IDEA Paper, 2005. Web. <https://www.ideaedu.org/Portals/0/Uploads/Documents/IDEA%20Papers/IDEA%20Papers/Idea_Paper_41.pdf >.
Svoboda, Frederic. "Landscapes Real and Imagined: 'Big Two-Hearted River.'" *Hemingway Review* 16.1 (1996): 33–42.
———. *Up North with the Hemingways and Nick Adams*. Mount Pleasant, MI: Clarke Historical Library, 2007.
Taylor, Diana. *The Archive and the Repertoire: Performing Cultural Memory in the Americas*. Durham: Duke UP, 2003.
Termine, Nancy, and Carroll Izard. "Infant's Responses to their Mothers' Expressions of Joy and Sadness." *Developmental Psychology* 24 (1988): 223–29.
Tooker, Dan, and Roger Hofheins. "Ernest J. Gaines." In Lowe. 99–111.
Toomer, Jean. *Cane*. 1923. New York: Liveright, 1993.
———. "Song of the Son." In Locke. 137.
Towne v. Eisner, 245 US 425. Supreme Court of the US. 1918.
Trogdon, Robert W. "'Forms of Combat': Hemingway, the Critics, and *Green Hills of Africa*." *Hemingway Review* 15.2 (1996): 1–14.
———. *The Lousy Racket: Hemingway, Scribners, and the Business of Literature*. Kent, OH: Kent State UP, 2007.
Trout, Steven. "'Where Do We Go from Here?': Ernest Hemingway's 'Soldier's Home' and American Veterans of World War I." *Hemingway Review* 20.1 (2000): 5–21.
Tyler, Lisa, ed. *Teaching Hemingway's* A Farewell to Arms. Kent, OH: Kent State UP, 2008.

West, Stan, et al. *Suburban Promised Land: The Emerging Black Community in Oak Park, Illinois, 1880–1980*. Oak Park, IL: Soweto West Press and The Historical Society of Oak Park and River Forest, 2009.

Wilentz, Gay. "(Re)Teaching Hemingway: Anti-Semitism as a Thematic Device in *The Sun Also Rises*." *College English* 52.2 (1990): 186–93.

Wintz, Cary D., ed. *Harlem Speaks: A Living History of the Harlem Renaissance*. Naperville, IL: Sourcebooks, 2007.

Wright-Cleveland, Margaret E. "*Cane* and *In Our* Time: A Literary Conversation about Race." In Holcomb and Scruggs. 151–76.

Selected Bibliography

Hemingway Texts

Hemingway, Ernest. *The Complete Short Stories of Ernest Hemingway: The Finca Vigía Edition.* New York: Scribner, 1987.
———. *Death in the Afternoon.* New York: Scribner, 1932.
———. *A Farewell to Arms.* New York: Scribner, 1995.
———. *Green Hills of Africa.* New York: Scribner, 1935.
———. *In Our Time.* New York: Boni and Liveright, 1925.
———. *A Moveable Feast: The Restored Edition.* New York: Scribner, 2010.
———. *The Sun Also Rises.* New York: Scribner, 1926.
———. *To Have and Have Not.* New York: Scribner, 1984.

Secondary Texts

Atkinson, Michael. *Hemingway Deadlights.* New York: St. Martin's, 2009.
Baker, Carlos. *Ernest Hemingway: A Life Story.* New York: Scribner, 1969.
———. *Hemingway, the Writer as Artist.* 4th ed. Princeton, NJ: Princeton UP, 1980.
Baker, Houston A., Jr. *Modernism and the Harlem Renaissance.* Chicago: U of Chicago P, 1987.
Balderrama, Francisco, and Raymond Rodríguez. *Decade of Betrayal: Mexican Repatriation in the 1930s.* Albuquerque: U of New Mexico P, 2016.
Bruccoli, Matthew J., ed. *The Only Thing That Counts: The Ernest Hemingway-Maxwell Perkins Correspondence.* Columbia: U of South Carolina P, 1996.
Capellán, Angel. *Hemingway and the Hispanic World.* Ann Arbor, MI: UMI Research Press, 1977.
Castro, Rafaela. *Chicano Folklore: A Guide To the Folktales, Traditions, Rituals, and Religious Practices of Mexican-Americans.* New York: Oxford UP, 2000.
Cowley, Malcolm. *Exile's Return: A Literary Odyssey of the 1920s.* New York: Viking Press, 1951.
Curnutt, Kirk. *Ernest Hemingway and the Expatriate Modernist Movement.* Detroit: Gale Group, 2000.
DeFalco, Joseph. *The Hero in Hemingway's Short Stories.* Pittsburgh: U of Pittsburgh P, 1963.

de Jongh, James. *Vicious Modernism: Black Harlem and the Literary Imagination*. New York: Cambridge UP, 1990.

Donaldson, Scott, ed. *The Cambridge Companion to Ernest Hemingway*. New York: Cambridge UP, 1996.

Douglas, Ann. *Terrible Honesty: Mongrel Manhattan in the 1920s*. New York: Farrar, Straus and Giroux, 1995.

Dudley, Marc. *Hemingway, Race, and Art: Bloodlines and the Color Line*. Kent, OH: Kent State UP, 2012.

Eby, Carl P. *Hemingway's Fetishism: Psychoanalysis and the Mirror of Manhood*. Albany: SUNY Press, 1999.

Fabre, Michel. *From Harlem to Paris: Black American Writers in France, 1840–1980*. Urbana: U of Illinois P, 1993.

Fetterley, Judith. *The Resisting Reader: A Feminist Approach to American Fiction*. Bloomington: Indiana UP, 1977.

Graff, Gerald. *Beyond the Culture Wars: How Teaching the Conflicts Can Revitalize American Education*. New York: Norton, 1992.

Holcomb, Gary Edward, and Charles Scruggs, eds. *Hemingway and the Black Renaissance*. Columbus: Ohio State UP, 2012.

Hughes, Langston. *The Collected Works of Langston Hughes, Volume 15: The Short Stories*. Ed. R. Baxter Miller. Columbia: U of Missouri P, 2002.

———. *I Wonder as I Wander: An Autobiographical Journey*. 1956. New York: Hill and Wang, 1993.

Kirschke, Amy Helene. *Aaron Douglas: Art, Race and the Harlem Renaissance*. Jackson: U of Mississippi P, 1995.

Kramsch, Claire. *Context and Culture in Language Teaching*. Oxford: Oxford UP, 1993.

Levinas, Emmanuel. *Ethics and Infinity: Conversations with Philippe Nemo*. Translated by Richard A. Cohen. Pittsburgh: Duquesne UP, 1985.

Lewis, David Levering. *When Harlem Was in Vogue*. New York: Knopf, 1981.

Mellow, James R. *Hemingway: A Life Without Consequences*. Boston: Houghton Mifflin, 1992.

Moddelmog, Debra A., and Suzanne del Gizzo, eds. *Ernest Hemingway in Context*. Cambridge: Cambridge UP, 2013.

Morrison, Toni. *Playing in the Dark: Whiteness and the Literary Imagination*. Cambridge, MA: Harvard UP, 1992.

Reynolds, Michael S. *Hemingway: The 1930s*. New York: Norton, 1997.

———. *The Young Hemingway*. New York: Blackwell, 1986.

Riley, Charles A. *The Jazz Age in France*. New York: Henry N. Abrams, 2004.

Stephens, Robert O. *Hemingway's Nonfiction: The Public Voice*. Chapel Hill: U of North Carolina P, 1968.

Stewart, Matthew. *Modernism and Tradition in Ernest Hemingway's In Our Time*. New York: Camden House, 2001.

Strong, Amy L. *Race and Identity in Hemingway's Fiction*. New York: Palgrave Macmillan, 2008.

Strychacz, Thomas. *Hemingway's Theaters of Masculinity*. Baton Rouge: Louisiana State UP, 2003.
Svoboda, Frederic. *Up North with the Hemingways and Nick Adams*. Mount Pleasant, MI: Clarke Historical Library, 2007.
Taylor, Diana. *The Archive and the Repertoire: Performing Cultural Memory in the Americas*. Durham: Duke UP, 2003.

Contributors

Cam Cobb is an associate professor in the faculty of education at the University of Windsor. His research interests include social justice in education, narrative pedagogy, and coteaching in adult learning contexts. His work has been published in such journals as *Per la Filosofia, Cinema: Philosophy and the Moving Image,* the *F. Scott Fitzgerald Review,* the *British Journal of Special Education,* the *International Journal of Bilingual Education and Bilingualism,* and the *International Journal of Inclusive Education.* Recently, he cowrote *Next to the Ice: Exploring the Culture and Community of Hockey in Canada.*

Mayuri Deka is an assistant professor and BA coordinator of the School of English Studies at the University of the Bahamas. She has published and presented numerous papers on American literature with a focus on multiethnic identities, postcolonial literatures, and pedagogy. She is in the process of writing a book on prosocial pedagogy and social justice. Deka has taught a wide range of classes on American and world literature, including surveys that include the study of Hemingway and his interactions with other cultures and races.

Sarah Driscoll is an English instructor at Phillips Academy-Andover. She has written reviews and articles on myriad topics, ranging from biopolitics in the work of Gabriel García Márquez to book reviews on photography of Ernest Hemingway and on nineteenth-century American life. Driscoll's master's thesis explored the relationship between Hemingway and modern Cuban painter Antonio Gattorno in letters discovered at the Hemingway Collection in the JFK Museum in Boston. In addition to her work on Hemingway and the Caribbean, Driscoll also specializes broadly in comparative literature, Latin American and Caribbean literature, and postcolonial New American studies. Over the years, Sarah has taught surveys in American literature, courses in composition, and courses that explore minority voices.

Marc Dudley (PhD, University of North Carolina) is an associate professor of twentieth-century American literature and African American literature in the Department of English, North Carolina State University. He has presented widely on race in the works of Ernest Hemingway, has published in *The Hemingway Review,* and is the author of *Bloodlines and the Color Line: Hemingway, Race, and Art* (Kent State University Press, 2012). Dudley has taught numerous literature and composition courses ranging from freshman composition to single-author seminars. Recent seminars include Ernest Hemingway and Idea(l)s of Acculturation and Blackness and the American Dream. His latest manuscript, *Understanding James Baldwin,* is forthcoming.

Gary Edward Holcomb is professor of African American Literature in the Department of African American Studies, Ohio University. With Charles Scruggs, he is coeditor of *Hemingway and the Black Renaissance,* a *Choice* Outstanding Title and Significant University Press Title for Undergraduates, and author of *Claude McKay, Code Name Sasha: Queer Black Marxism and the Harlem Renaissance.* In 2016 Holcomb was an NEH Humanities Summer Visiting Scholar at the Ernest J. Gaines Center Summer Institute, University of Louisiana, where he talked on the intertextual dialogue between the "Two Ernests," Hemingway and Gaines.

Joshua M. Murray (PhD, Kent State University) is assistant professor of English at Fayetteville State University. His scholarship focuses primarily on African American literature with an emphasis on the Harlem Renaissance. His publications examine works from a range of authors, including Nella Larsen, Jessie Redmon Fauset, Walter F. White, and Toni Morrison. Murray has taught a variety of English courses on topics such as African American literature, twentieth-century American literature, critical theory, and composition. He has also taught an interdisciplinary colloquium titled "Race in America," which explores relevant literary and cultural movements of America's past and present.

Candice L. Pipes was most recently the head of the Department of English and Fine Arts at the United States Air Force Academy, Colorado. She has taught courses on 1920's American literature, violence against women in literature, and protest literature. Her scholarly pursuits focus on representations of violence against women in African American literature and the expression of the trauma of war in literature.

Michael K. Potter is a teaching and learning specialist in the Centre for Teaching and Learning at the University of Windsor. His research focuses on applications of pragmatist, anarchist, and nihilist philosophy in higher education. Publications include *Bertrand Russell's Ethics* (2006) and *Leading Effective Discussions* (with Erika Kustra, 2008). He was coeditor of a special issue of the *Canadian Journal for the Scholarship of Teaching and Learning* in 2015, which focused on the neglected role of the arts and humanities in the scholarship of teaching and learning.

Ross K. Tangedal is assistant professor of English at the University of Wisconsin–Stevens Point. He specializes in twentieth-century American print and publishing culture, book history, and textual editing, with emphases on Ernest Hemingway, F. Scott Fitzgerald, and Midwestern literature. His work has been published in the *Hemingway Review*, the *F. Scott Fitzgerald Review*, *Authorship*, *MidAmerica*, *Midwestern Miscellany*, *Teaching Hemingway and the Natural World* (Kent State UP), and *A Scattering Time: How Modernism Met Midwestern Culture*. His edition of John Herrmann's *Foreign Born* was published in 2018 (Hastings College Press), and he is at work on a book manuscript focused on authorial prefaces in American writing. He is a contributing editor for the Hemingway Letters Project (Cambridge UP) and a member of the Hemingway Society's Advisory Council for Younger Scholars.

Matthew Teutsch is an instructor of English at Auburn University. He has published in *MELUS: Multi-Ethnic Literature of the United States*, *Mississippi Quarterly*, *Studies in the Literary Imagination*, and *Literature of the Early American Republic: Annual Studies on Cooper and His Contemporaries*. He also has various book chapters on Ernest J. Gaines, George Washington Cable, Charles Chesnutt, Robert Beck, and others. Teutsch served as the interim director of the Ernest J. Gaines Center and served as codirector of the 2016 NEH Summer Institute "Ernest J. Gaines and the Southern Experience." He maintains *Interminable Rambling*, a blog about literature, culture, pedagogy, and composition studies.

Margaret E. Wright-Cleveland is the director of Faculty Development at Florida State University. In 2015–16 she served as a Fulbright Scholar to Côte d'Ivoire where she taught in the English Department of Université Félix Houphouët-Boigny and researched Bernard Binlin Dadié. In West Africa she taught American poetry, *Adventures of Huckleberry Finn*, and *My Jim* to lycée 3 and graduate students whose third language was English. In the United States, Wright-Cleveland has taught a plethora of freshman composition courses, as well as upper division and graduate courses in American studies, American literature, and women's studies to native English speakers rarely in possession of a third language. Margaret has published essays on Hemingway in *MidAmerica*, *Hemingway and the Black Renaissance*, and *Teaching Hemingway and Modernism*.

Index

abortion, 91–92
Active Learning, 22, 25, 27–28, 53–54
Adams, Dr., 26, 27, 55, 56, 60; Boulton and, 57
Adams, Nick, 3, 6, 9, 10, 14, 26, 55, 56, 93, 116, 117; Ad and, 13; bucolic world of, 120; Bugs and, 13; George and, 95; grasshoppers and, 119; impressions of, 12–13; modernity and, 122; Ojibwe and, 46; portrayal of, 118; whiteness and, 26
Adventures of Huckleberry Finn, The (Twain), 110, 112
Africa Dip (game), 21
African American authors, 96, 97
African Americans, 6, 10, 18, 90, 108; interpretation of, 92; place of, 117
African Communities League, 86
African Dodger (game), 21
Africanist presence, 107, 112
alienation, 70, 76, 78, 80, 83, 84, 95, 117; cultural, 109; social, 105, 109
American Dream, 80, 97n1, 101
American GI Forum (AGIF), 83
American Home Missionary Society, 19
American Missionary Association, 19
American Studies, 3, 17
Andreson, Ole, 3
anti-Mexican hysteria, 75
anti-Semitism, 106, 112
art: adjustment and, 34; Black American, 92, 96; modernist, 86; Negro, 96
Artifact Annotated Bibliography, 22, 25
artifacts, 70–71
Ashley, Lady Brett, 107, 108, 111
"Author," "Old Lady" and, 32
avant-garde movement, 109
Avey, 6, 117–18, 120, 122
"Avey" (Toomer), 6, 115, 117

background: cultural, 62; objectives and, 42–43
Baker, Carlos, 41, 91, 92
Balderrama, Francisco, 75
Ballantine Ale, 45

Banjo (McKay), 108
Banks, James: model of, 59, 60
Baraka, Amiri, 87
Barnard, Kate, 24, 25
Barnard, Rita, 86, 88
Barnes, Jake, 38, 46, 107, 108
Barton, William E., 20
Batson, Daniel, 44
"Battler, The" (Hemingway), 2–3, 9, 10, 118; racial politics and, 15n1; teaching, 7–8, 14
Bay View Association, 23
Bay View Chautauqua, 23, 28n5
Bayonne, 116, 121, 122; racism/oppression in, 117, 120
Bayonne, Auntie, 121
Bayonne, Monsieur, 121
Belmonte, Juan, 30, 31, 32–33, 34
Bennett, Gwendolyn, 2, 6, 109, 110, 112
Benson, Jackson, 93
Beyond the Culture Wars (Graff), 43
"Big Two-Hearted River" (Hemingway), 6, 115, 116, 118
Biggs, John, 53, 64
bigotry, 77, 83
binary oppositions, 86, 91
Birth of a Nation, The (Griffith), 11
black body, 94, 95
black boxer, 109, 110, 111, 112
black characters, treatment of, 111
Black codes, repeal of, 19
black community, 20, 28, 95
black man, double vision of, 117
Blackbird, Andrew J., 23, 24, 28n7
blackness, 87, 94, 96; ideology of, 90; views of, 16, 20; whiteness and, 3, 17, 21–22
Bloody Summer (1919), 86–87
Bloom, Benjamin, 58
Bloom's Revised Taxonomy, 4, 57, 58–59
Bones of the Others, The (Justice), 39
Boulton, Dick, 26–27, 55, 56, 60; Adams and, 57
Boulton, Eddy, 55
Bowling Alone (Putnam), 41

136

Bracher, Mark, 44
Bransford, J. D., 65
Bredendick, Nancy, 30
Brenner, Anita, 81
Brown, A. L., 65
Bugs, 2–3, 9, 10, 12; Ad and, 13, 14, 118; Nick and, 13
bullfighters, 30, 33, 40, 93–94, 111; audience of, 34; treatment of, 31–32
bullfighting, 31, 34, 39, 45, 99; apologia for, 35; ritual, 31–32
Bureau of Immigration, 82
Burhans, Clinton, 88, 93
"Butterfly and the Tank, The" (Hemingway), 98

Cajuns, 121
Callaghan, Morley, 74
Campbell, Mike, 107
Cane (Toomer), 115, 116, 117
"Capital of the World, The" (Hemingway), 29
Catherine Carmier (Gaines), 114
Cecilia, Sister, 77, 78
Chautauqua, 23, 28n5
Chicago Women's Club, 19
Chicanos, 5, 83, 84
Chickering, A. W., 65
Chicuelo, 32
Chippewa, 23
"City of Refuge, The" (Fisher), 89
civil rights bill, 19
Cobb, Cam, 4
Cocking, R. R., 65
code heroes, 13, 46
Cohn, Robert, 106, 107, 111
Collis, K. F., 64
color line, 90
complex pastoralism, 116–17
constructivism, 54, 64, 72, 73n2
consumer culture, production culture and, 86
Cooper, Stephen, 102
Cowley, Malcolm, 95
create, 58, 59, 60, 61, 62
Critical Race Theory, 17, 83, 84
critical thinking skills, 58
"Cross Country Snow" (Hemingway), 95
Cullen, Countee, 96, 107
culminating reflection activity, 71–72
cultural community, 80
cultural labeling, 106
cultural presence, 17
cultural space, 46
culture, 70, 86; Afro-American, 90; American, 16–17, 28, 46, 102; Basque, 105; consumer, 86; encounters with, 45–48; historical, 17; identification with, 46; language and, 42;
Mexican, 79, 82; Other, 46; production, 86; race and, 45–48, 47, 50; school, 59; white, 56; youth, 95
Curnutt, Kirk, 86, 87, 88, 89, 92, 96; expatriate modernism and, 95

Damon, William, 43
Dangerous Summer, The (Hemingway), 29–30
Darder, Antonia, 59
De Jongh, James: on Harlem, 89
De la Haba, Antonio, 33
De la Haba, Manuel, 33
De la Palma, Niño, 32
Death in the Afternoon (Hemingway) (*DIA*), 30, 31–35, 38, 39; bullfighting and, 34; matadors in, 36; misreading of, 40; quote from, 29
Deka, Mayuri, 4
deportation laws, 75
derive, 58, 59, 60, 61, 62
desegregation, 19, 43
Dewey, John, 54, 64
DIA. See *Death in the Afternoon* (Hemingway) (*DIA*)
Dingley Tariff Act (1897), 75
discrimination, 11, 19, 78, 83, 121
diversity, 15n3, 42, 43; racial, 41
"Doctor and the Doctor's Wife, The" (Hemingway) (*TDDW*), 4, 22, 25, 26, 55–57, 59; Active Learning and, 54; learning outcomes for, 53, 58; publication of, 53; racial identity and, 60; reading, 63, 64, 66, 67, 69, 70, 72; social context report for, 71
Donovan, S., 65
Dos Passos, John, 86, 97n1
double vision, 117, 120
Douglas, Aaron: on African American art, 92
Douglas, Ann, 88, 89, 93, 94, 95
Doyle, Jack, 15n2
Driscoll, Sarah, 5
Droopy, 29, 30, 31, 36, 37, 38
Du Bois, W. E. B.: on color line, 90
Dudley, Kevin: on Boulton, 57
Dudley, Marc, 2, 30, 35, 36, 39
Dunbar, Paul Laurence, 96

Eby, Carl P., 45, 52n3
economic crisis, 5, 82, 86, 98
economic status, 71
education, 70; banking concept of, 54; multicultural, 59; problem-posing, 54; racial, 17, 18, 25, 27
Elizabeth Charleton Day Nursery, 21
Ellison, Ralph, 2
empathy: circle of, 49, 51; for Other, 44, 47, 50, 51; secure, 43–44

Epstein, Reese N., 115
equality, 122; racial, 16, 19–20, 21
Ernest Hemingway and the Expatriate Modernist Movement (Curnutt), 88
Ernest Hemingway: Machismo and Masochism (Fantina), 1
Esquire, 99
eugenics, 11
evaluate, 58, 59, 60, 61, 62
expatriate literature/writers, 88–89, 95, 97
experiences, 22, 49, 53; learner-centered, 73; learning, 55, 60–61, 62, 63
Extended Abstract, 64

Fabre, Michel, 107, 112
Fairclough, Norman: on human interaction, 8–9
Fantina, Richard, 1
Farewell to Arms, A (Hemingway), 10, 41, 45, 46, 47, 48; identity and, 51
Farewell to Arms, A (movie), 50
Faulkner, William, 1, 114
Fauset, Jessie, 107
feedback, 44, 54, 62, 65, 71
Fetterley, Judith, 43
fiction: reading, 45; reality and, 45; suspicion of, 44–45
"Fight to Preserve Land to Papooses Who Are the Prey of 'Land Grafters'" (*Petoskey News*), 24
First Congregational Church, 20
Fisher, Rudolph, 89
Fitzgerald, F. Scott, 86, 97n1
For Whom the Bell Tolls (Hemingway), 10, 29, 46
Forest Park Amusement Park, 21
Francis, Ad, 10; Bugs and, 13, 14, 118; impressions of, 12–13; Nick and, 13
Francis, Adolph, 9
Frazer, 76, 77, 78; Cayetano and, 79–80; music and, 81; on poverty, 79
Freire, Paulo, 54
From Harlem to Paris: Black American Writers in France, 1840–1980 (Fabre), 107, 112

Gaines, Ernest J., 6, 114, 115–16, 120; complex pastoralism and, 116–17; oppressive society and, 121–22
"Gambler, the Nun, and the Radio, The" (Hemingway), 74, 75, 76; teaching, 82–83, 84
Gamson, Z. F., 65
Garcia, Manuel, 33
Garland, Hamlin, 86
Garvey, Marcus, 86
gender roles, 42, 52n3, 70, 106, 107

George, Uncle, 26
Gibson, Willard P., 28n7
Gillis, King Solomon, 89
Gorton, Bill, 106, 110, 111
Graff, Gerald, 43
Granero, Manuel, 32
grasshoppers, black, 119, 119–20, 121
Great Depression, 75, 80; Mexican workers and, 75–76, 84
Great Gatsby, The (Fitzgerald), 97n1
Great Migration, 117
Green Hills of Africa (Hemingway), 15n1, 30, 46, 110; misreading of, 40; modern American literature and, 112; narrative/memory and, 29; quote from, 29; significance of, 35–39
Griffith, D. W., 11
Gross, Ariela J., 83

Harlem, 85, 87, 89, 92, 97
Harlem Renaissance, 2, 5, 6, 85, 86, 87, 88, 96, 97, 107, 108, 109, 110, 111, 115; announcement of, 9
Hathaway, Albert, 28n7
Hediger, Ryan, 30
Hemingway and Gellhorn (movie), 45–46
"Hemingway and McKay, Race and Nation" (Holcomb), 108, 112
Hemingway and the Black Renaissance (Holcomb and Scruggs), 2, 99
Hemingway, Anson, 18
Hemingway, Ernest: artistic dexterity of, 30–31; authorial character of, 40; experimentation by, 15n1, 39; influence of, 28; legacy of, 14; popularity of, 28; racial education of, 19, 22, 25, 30–31; racism of, 11, 106. *See also individual works*
Hemingway, Race, and Art: Bloodlines and Color Lines (Dudley), 1–2, 39
"Hemingway Story, A" (Hughes), 98
Hemingway's Reading (Reynolds), 10
Hemingway's Theaters of Masculinity (Strychacz), 39
Henry, Frederick, 48
Himes, Chester, 2
Historical Society of Oak Park and River Forest, 28n1
history: cultural, 18; reality of, 116
History of the Ottawa and Chippewa Indians of Michigan (Blackbird), 23
Hoff, Hild E., 45
Hoffman, Frederick J., 101
Holcomb, Gary Edward, 6, 99, 100
Holmes, Oliver, 12
"Home" (Hughes), 6, 99, 100, 104
Home to Harlem (McKay), 6, 108, 109, 112
"How to Overcome Race Prejudice" (West), 19

Howard Glee Club, 117
Hughes, Langston, 2, 5–6, 8, 94–95, 96, 98, 100, 101, 102, 104, 107, 108; poetic style of, 99; racism and, 103
hunting, 31, 39; durability/brotherhood and, 37; ideology, 35
Hurston, Zora Neale, 8, 85, 114

"I, Too" (Hughes), 94
I Wonder as I Wander (Hughes), 98, 100
Iceberg Theory, 109
identify, 58, 60, 61, 62
identity, 4, 23, 25, 28, 35, 41, 46; competing, 91; complex, 42, 51; construction of, 22; development, 42; empathetic, 48; ethnic, 34; racial, 19, 32, 52n1, 54, 57, 60, 103; secure, 42, 43, 44, 48, 51; Self and, 44; self-articulated, 111; structures, 47
ideology, 1, 90, 92, 96; hunting, 35; imperialist, 36; masculinist, 112; racist, 102
"If I Must Die" (McKay), 87
immigrants, 6, 41; Latin American, 5
immigration laws, 75, 82
imperialism, 3, 35, 36, 40
In Our Time (Hemingway), 3, 6, 10, 11, 25–28, 28n8, 39, 88, 93, 99, 110, 115; teaching, 16, 17, 85, 86
"Indian Camp" (Hemingway), 18, 22, 25, 26, 72
"Indian" Society, 26
"Indians Moved Away, The" (Hemingway), 72
inequity, 18, 59, 85
Ingalls, Charles W., 28n7
integration, 2, 65, 92; content, 59; racial, 19; social, 19

James, 6, 116, 120, 122; segregation and, 121
Jazz Age, 105–6, 107, 108, 109
Jefferson, Augustine, 114
Jews, 46
Jim Crow, 11, 83, 94, 111
Jim (slave), 110
Johnson, Jack, 11, 14
Johnston, Kenneth G., 98
Jones, Gayl, 2
Jordan, Robert, 46
Joselito, 32
Joyce, James, 114
Justice, Hilary K., 30, 39

Kansas City Star, 10
Karsh, Yousuf, 114
Kazin, Alfred, 87
"Killers, The" (Hemingway), racist language in, 3
Kinnamon, Kenneth, 15n1

Kirschke, Amy Helene, 92
knowledge, 54; biased, 49; construction, 59; decontextualized, 54
Kramsch, Claire, 45
Krathwohl, David, 58
Krebs, Harold, 99, 100, 101–2; conflict of, 102–3; displacement of, 88–89
Ku Klux Klan, 86, 111

"La Cucaracha" (song), 81
Lalanda, Marcial, 32
landscapes, 39; authoritative, 81; historical, 82; racial, 12, 86
Langston Hughes: A Study of the Short Fiction (Ostrom), 103
language, 57, 70, 112; culture and, 42; Mexican, 82; power of, 18; racial, 2–3; Spanish, 46, 81; temporal nature of, 12
Language and Power (Fairclough), 8–9
Larsen, Steen F., 45
Latin American countries, 82, 84
Latino population, growth of, 83
learning: active project-oriented, 65; context, 61–62; facilitating, 63; judging, 63; scaffolding, 62–63; social justice, 57
learning outcomes, 54–55, 65; complex, 62; demonstrating, 69; developing, 53, 57–58, 59, 60, 64; experiences and, 60–61
Lee, William H., 28n7
Leigh, David, 93–94
Lewis, David Levering, 85, 96
literary analysis, 60, 61, 62–63, 64, 69; conducting, 58
literature: African American, 115; black, 87, 99; role of, 44–45; studying, 61
Locke, Alain LeRoy, 6, 84, 85, 90–91, 92; McKay and, 91; Negro youth and, 96; on Younger Generation, 96
lost generation, 105, 106, 107, 110, 112, 113
"Lost Generation Negrotarians," 85
Lounsberry, Barbara, 30
Lousy Racket, The (Trogdon), 39
LULAC, 83
lynchings, 11, 100, 110, 111, 112

Machine in the Garden, The (Marx), 116
MacKethan, Lucinda H.: on Toomer, 117
MacLeish, Archibald, 75, 74S
Maera, 31, 94
Maier, Kevin, 30, 35
"Mandarlo al carajo," 76
Mandel, Miriam, 30
Manhattan Transfer (Dos Passos), 97n1
manhood-fashioning, drama of, 35
Marshall, Ian, 119

Marshall, Paule, 108
Martínez, George, 83
Marx, Leo: complex pastoral and, 116
Masai, 37, 38
masculinity: American, 52n3; black, 111, 112; Jewish, 112
matadors, 32–33, 33–34, 36
Mayer, Richard, 54
McKay, Claude, 2, 6, 94, 96, 107, 108, 109, 112, 114; Locke and, 91; poem by, 87, 90
M'Cola, 29, 30, 31, 36, 37, 38, 39; wardrobe of, 40
Melling, Philip, 119
Mellow, James, 46–47
Melville, Herman, 1
Methodist Church, Bay View Association and, 23
Mexican Revolution, 81
Mexicans, 6; alienation of, 83; Great Depression and, 75–76, 84; labor of, 75, 83; in Montana, 74–82; music and, 81; poverty of, 79; racial profiling and, 82
Milanese Barber, 48
Miller, William H., 28n7
minimalism, 2, 99
minorities: ethnic, 113; perspectives of, 43; racial, 42
"Minstrel Man" (Hughes), 94–95
modern American literature, source of, 112
modernism, 6, 85–86, 92; American, 87, 104, 105; expatriate, 86, 88, 95–96; Negro, 87; New Negro, 88, 95–96
modernists, 86, 115; black, 85, 89, 92; expatriate, 96; white, 2, 85, 89, 96. *See also* New Negro modernists
Montmartre, 105, 109
Morrice, James L., 28n7
Morrison, Toni, 1, 8, 12, 106–7, 112
Mt. Caramel Baptist Church, 19, 20
Moveable Feast, A (Hemingway), 10, 41, 45, 46, 48, 50; identity and, 47, 51
"Mr. and Mrs. Elliot" (Hemingway), 89–90
Multiple Lens Portfolio, 53, 61, 62, 63–65, 72, 73n5
Murray, Albert, 2
Murray, Joshua M., 5, 6
music, 16, 23, 80, 82, 100; Mexicans and, 81

N-word, 10–11, 12, 110. *See also* nigger
Native Americans, 18, 27, 46, 46–47, 119
Negro: objectification of, 103; term/usage of, 12
"Negro Youth Speaks" (Locke), 96
New Negro, 89, 92, 93, 96, 107; characters, 108–9
New Negro, The (Locke), 6, 89, 94, 96; fiction/visual art from, 88; foreword to, 90–91; modernist style of, 92; morality/Puritanical values and, 90; reading, 85, 86
New Negro modernists, 92, 94, 95–96, 109, 111
New York Times, 75

Newkirk, C. F., 28n7
nigger, 13, 105, 106, 111, 112; usage of term, 12. *See also* N-word
Nigger Jim, 110
Nineteenth Century Club, 20–21

Oak Leaves, 16, 21, 28n2
Oak Park, Illinois, 11, 15n3, 16, 25, 28; African Americans in, 18; historical culture of, 17; historical look at, 22; as racialized community, 18–22; racism in, 21, 25
Oak Park-River Forest Boys Choir, 20
Oatley, Keith: on fiction, 44–45
O'Connor, Flannery, 9
Octavia, 6, 116, 120, 121, 122
Ojibwe, 23, 24, 26, 46, 55, 56, 60, 73n3; English and, 57; portrayal of, 69, 70, 71, 72
"Old Lady," "Author" and, 32
Old Man and the Sea, The (Hemingway), 29
Old Zurito, 31, 33, 40
"On the Quai at Smyrna" (Hemingway), 28n8
oppression, 6, 80, 117, 122
Ostrom, Hans, 103
Other, 26, 52, 101; cultural, 2, 49, 50; empathy for, 44, 47, 50, 51; identification with, 46, 47; racial, 48, 49, 50; Self and, 4, 42, 43–44, 45, 47, 48, 49, 50, 51; suffering of, 42, 44
Ott, Mark P., 98
"Our Indebtedness to Negroes for Their Conduct during the War" (West), 19
"Out of Season" (Hemingway), 91, 92
outcomes, 61; components of, 63; enriching, 58–59
ownership, 46, 56, 60, 94

Palmer, Will, 19
Pan-Africanist movements, 92
Paris Noir (Stovall), 108, 112
pedagogy, 30, 31, 42, 43, 44, 51, 83; constructivist, 64; critical, 59–61, 64, 72, 73, 73n6; equitable, 59; feminist, 61; multicultural, 105
Pentecost, Jack, 119
Perkins, Maxwell, 28n8, 35, 37
Petoskey, Michigan, 16; historical culture of, 17; racial education in, 18, 22–25; racism in, 25
Petoskey News, 24
Pflug, Melissa A.: on ethics, 24
phrenology, 11
Pipes, Candice, 5, 6
Plath, James, 98
Playing in the Dark: Whiteness and the Literary Imagination (Morrison), 1, 12, 106–7, 112
politics, 9, 83, 96; racial, 4, 8, 15n1, 42; Self/Other, 4, 42
portfolio learning reflection, 71–72
post-traumatic stress disorder (PTSD), 86,

94, 103
Potter, Michael K., 4
poverty, 79, 102
power, 23, 25, 47, 54, 60
prejudice, 47, 49, 59, 121
progressivism, 19, 25
prosocial behavior, 42, 43, 51
PTSD. *See* post-traumatic stress disorder (PTSD)
Puritanism, 90
Putnam, Robert D., 41

R-word, 11
race, 1, 60, 100, 116; American culture and, 16–17; complication of, 30; contextualizing, 2, 4, 31, 40; conversation about, 18, 27; culture and, 45–48, 50; encounters with, 45–48, 122; reading through, 8
Race and Identity in Hemingway's Fiction (Strong), 1
race relations, 14, 44, 119
race riots, 86–87
racial construction, 17, 22, 28
racial difference, 30, 57
racial epithets, 11, 12
racial issues, 86, 87, 106
racial markers, 12, 27, 57, 106
racial profiling, 5, 82, 84
racism, 3, 6, 11, 21, 25, 80, 83, 84, 88, 100, 101, 102, 103, 106, 110, 117, 121, 122; combatting, 90; critique of, 76–77; experiencing, 22; military, 108; slavery and, 120; whiteness and, 22
racists, 102, 103, 106
Reconstruction, 19, 94
"Red Summer, The," 15n3, 119
Reese, Miss, 103
Reflective Review Discussion, 68
reflective thinking, 64
Reiss, Winold, 92
relate, 58, 59, 60, 61, 62
religion, 71; poor and, 79
"Return of the Native" (Baraka), 87
Reynolds, Michael, 10, 21, 36
Richardson, Hadley, 28n3
Rieser, Andrew C.: whiteness and, 23
Rodríguez, Raymond, 75
Romero, Pedro, 111
Rowell, Charles, 121
Roy, Joseph E., 18–19
Ruiz, Cayetano, 76; Frazer and, 79–80; music and, 81; Sister Cecilia and, 77, 78
rural, urban and, 117–18

St. James, 47
St. Vincent Hospital, 74

Sandburg, Carl: Chicago and, 15n3
Schmalzbauer, Leah, 83
Scribner, 14, 28n8
Scribner's Magazine, 74
Scruggs, Charles, 99, 100
segregation, 19, 43, 83, 121
Seilman, Uffe, 45
Self: identity and, 44; Other and, 4, 42, 43–44, 45, 47, 48, 49, 51; sense of, 44, 50
self-image, 43
self-realization, 94
self-referral effect, 65
Seney, 6, 116, 118, 119, 122
"Seven Principles for Good Practice in Undergraduate Education" (Chickering and Gamson), 65
Seventieth U.S. Colored Troops, 18
sex issues, 90, 105, 106, 107
Shaffer, Donald M., Jr., 116, 117, 118
"Short Happy Life of Francis Macomber" (Hemingway), 30
Singer, Peter: Other and, 45
"Sky Is Gray, The" (Gaines), 6, 116, 117, 118, 120
slavery, 94, 110, 115; racism and, 120
social actions, 44, 59
social betterment, 20–21
social capital, 41, 43
social context, 54, 61, 69–70, 70–71
social justice, 62, 82; learning, 57; thinking, 72
sociological dimensions, 8, 56, 59, 60, 72
"Soldier's Home" (Hemingway), 6, 88, 99, 100, 101, 104, 117
"Song of the Sun" (Toomer), 94
southern pastoral, 117, 118
Southwestern Review, 115
spicks, 76, 77, 82
Stein, Gertrude, 37, 105
Steinbeck, John, 80, 114
Stephens, Robert O., 36
stereotypes, 3, 17, 25, 36, 95, 106
Stewart, Matthew, 90
Stewart, Michael, 91–92, 95
story maps, 66–68, 68–69, 71
Stovall, Tyler, 108, 112
Strong, Amy L., 1, 30, 57
Structure of Observed Learning Outcomes (SOLO), 64
Strychacz, Thomas, 30, 34, 35, 37, 39, 56
Suburban Promised Land (West), 28n1
sugar-beet workers, 75, 76
Sun Also Rises, The (Hemingway), 6, 10, 29, 46, 105, 106, 107, 108, 111; *afición* in, 38; Africanist presence in, 112; black boxer in, 109, 110; modern American literature and, 112
Svinicki, M. D., 65
Svoboda, Frederic J., 118

Tabeshaw, Billy, 55, 56
Tang, C.: transformative reflection and, 64
Tangedal, Ross K., 3–4
TDDW. See "Doctor and the Doctor's Wife, The" (Hemingway) (*TDDW*)
"Ten Indians" (Hemingway), 72
Teutsch, Matthew, 6
text: context and, 48; teaching, 82–83
thinking, 57; higher-order, 58; prosocial, 52
Thurman, Wallace, 2
To Have and Have Not (Hemingway), 15n1, 82
Tolstoy, Leo, 114
Toomer, Jean, 6, 94, 116, 118, 122; double vision and, 120; Hemingway and, 115
Toronto Star, 10
transformation, 64, 86, 121
transplanting, analogy of, 47
Triangular Road (Marshall), 108
Trogdon, Robert W., 30, 36, 39
Trout, Steven, 101
True at First Light (Hemingway), 29
Turgenev, Ivan, 114
Twain, Mark, 110, 112
Tyler, Lisa, 30

"Undefeated, The" (Hemingway), 29, 33
Under Kilimanjaro (Hemingway), 10, 29
Unity Church, 19
Universal Negro Improvement Association, 86
urban, rural and, 117–18

Vallée, Rudy, 74
violence, 9, 10, 12, 13, 57, 60, 80, 85, 93, 95, 101; racial, 11, 15n3, 21, 22, 87, 103

Wakamba tribe, 46
Walcott, Derek, 2
Walker, Al, 119
Washington, Booker T.: racial equality and, 21
Watson, Paul, 109, 110

Ways of White Folks, The (Hughes), 99
"Wedding Day" (Bennett), 6, 109, 110, 112
Wells-Barnett, Ida B.: racial equality and, 21
White and McNally Company, 27, 55, 56
"White House, The" (McKay), 90, 91
"White Houses" (Locke). *See* "White House, The" (McKay)
white man, 26, 27, 57
white privilege, 25, 26, 27
white supremacists, 1, 84, 87, 105, 111, 112
whiteness, 26, 39, 87; blackness and, 3, 17, 21–22; integration of, 2; legal definitions of, 83; privilege of, 16, 21; racism and, 22; social understanding of, 23; views of, 20
Wilentz, Gay: on alien population, 46
Williams, Fannie Barrier, 19
Williams, Roy, 99–100, 101, 104; crime of, 103; trauma of, 102
Wilson, Edmund, 28n8
Wittman, Emily, 30
Wolgast, Adolph, 15n2
Women's National Indian Association, 23
Women's Studies, 3, 17
word/emotion pairings, 51
World War I, 48, 86, 93, 99, 119; consequences of, 94; disillusionment of, 41; racism during, 108
wounds, 38, 79; textual/actual, 37; tribal, 37
Wright, Charles R., 28n7
Wright, Frances, 20
Wright, Frank Lloyd, 20
Wright, Richard, 2, 8, 114
Wright-Cleveland, Margaret E., 3, 115
writer's checklist, 68–69
writing style, 54, 115

Young Zurito, 31, 33

Zelli, 105, 109
Zuritos, 30, 31, 33, 34, 35, 38, 40

www.ingramcontent.com/pod-product-compliance
Lightning Source LLC
Chambersburg PA
CBHW021145230426
43667CB00005B/257